Seven-Minute Transformational Journal

Seven-Minute Transformational Journal

Seven minutes a day:
The experiment that could change your life

Sheila (Day) Shaver, BCND, CNHP, CHCC, C.HP

ISBN-13: 978-1-6886-0569-5

Printed in the United States of America

Publication Date: September 30, 2019

This journal is dedicated to
all of my amazing mentors, friends,
colleagues, clients, and family members
who encouraged and supported me as I
overcame so much and who had a part
in my beautiful transformation.

~~~

This journal is also dedicated to
those who are curious about what is still in store,
those who are earnestly seeking answers and truths,
those who are ready to take responsibility for their life,
those who are adventurous and willing to experiment,
those who want to touch the world in a positive way
and leave your healing signature for others.

My letter to you...

I am excited that you have chosen to use this journal, and I hope to hear from you once you have completed it. While I cannot make any promises or guarantees, as your results always depend upon your own decisions and actions. What I want you to know is that this journal is the product of a life-changing experiment I did myself and then feeling led by the Lord to help others transform their lives by what I learned. Please share your experience with me at:
7minutetransformationaljournal@gmail.com.

I want to start by telling you that you are here on earth for a very unique purpose. You were created to be an original, unlike anyone else! If you live life finding fault with yourself and feeling you should be like someone else or wishing you were, you will cheat yourself, your family, your community, and the world of the precious gift of "you". I spent most of my life wishing I were more like someone else, wishing I looked like "that", wishing I could do "that", wishing I had "that", etc. What a sad and uncomfortable life that was. What I did not realize was, my focus on everything 'wrong' (or what I perceived to be wrong) kept me in a negative field, kept me from appreciating who I was, kept me from feeling free to be me, kept me from accomplishing what I was created to accomplish.

As one who has experienced many very difficult, painful, and even seriously traumatic life events, I feel I have a great deal of understanding of what it means to have devastating challenges to overcome. I have learned through it all that I actually get to choose how I respond to things and that what I tell myself about it will determine how I feel about it. For instance, you and I can go through the exact same event and come out feeling completely different about it based on what we tell ourselves. What some people find devastating and awful, others will find an opportunity or learning experience. While some people choose to become bitter in their disappointments, others will choose to become better and overcome.

And you may say, "but you have no idea how horrible things have been." Yes, I used to say that myself, until I finally realized how much power I had and that I was responsible for my responses. After spending most of my life feeling powerless and victimized and drawing more of the things I did not want, I finally learned that I was exactly where I was because of choices I made. While we cannot control what others do to us, we can control what we do about it. We can be a 'victim' or we can become empowered.

The Word says in 2 Corinthians 10:5 to "....take captive every thought," which means that we cannot control the thoughts that may come to us, but we can control what we do with them. Proverbs 23:7 says "For as he thinketh in his heart, so is he." Wow, that one really got me to thinking. Could that really mean that I can be whatever I want to be? If that is true, then I cannot blame anyone or anything for what I am or am not. God says that whatever "I" think, so I am. Well this sure brings a great deal of responsibility and accountability.

In further exploration of all of this, one of my mentors suggested developing a practice of gratitude journaling. I was not really a fan of journaling, but I found one that actually led me to write responses, so I was not on my own trying to figure out what I should write about. I began the exercise while also building my own business without the experience, knowledge, or tools to do so, just the determination. As I was transitioning from working many years as a Paramedic and schooling in natural medicine to building a practice as a naturopath, I was also rebuilding my life mentally, physically, emotionally after some very devastating events that nearly ended my life. I wanted desperately to be truly free, empowered, successful, healthy, and happy so I listened to those who had already attained it.

While I did not really notice all the subtle changes initially, I did begin to notice a transformation inside of me as I took time every morning upon waking and every night before going to sleep to "take captive every thought" and begin to direct them. I decided if it was not getting me closer to my goal, if it was not offering me life, success, health, happiness, then it had to be replaced with what would. As my entire life began transforming, my mental and emotional wounds healing, my relationships healing, my business flourishing, my finances improving, my health improving, I felt I was finally where I was intended to be all along but kept myself from. Then, "life happened"... things got very busy and I stopped my daily morning and bedtime practices. Within weeks it felt like things were going backwards and within several months I found myself far from where I had just come. I finally realized what was going on, that I had not been directing my thoughts intentionally and had fallen back into some old habits of thinking without even realizing it.

I got back to my daily practices and within weeks I was back in forward motion. That was monumental for me, to see what a difference it really makes when we "take captive every thought" and are intentional about what we think and how we think. So, I have proven that we truly do have the power within us to create whatever we want, that we truly are responsible for how our lives turn out and that "For as he thinketh in his heart, so is he" is absolute truth! What power we have that many may never realize.

This journal has been created to give everyone the opportunity to do the experiment for themselves. My desire is to help others become empowered, as so many precious influential people have helped me to become. My desire is to help others believe in themselves, to appreciate who they were created to be, to learn to love and nourish the amazing and unique individual they are, to help them experience freedom and contentment, to start writing their story the way the want it to be, and to realize the ability they have to add value to others lives.

I want to challenge you to take this Seven-Minute Transformational Journal as a serious experiment and then share with me your amazing transformational stories at: **7minutetransformationaljournal@gmail.com**. As you continue your practice of journaling, please share your experiences and transformations with others to encourage them to do the experiment for themselves so they can enjoy a transformed life as well. May we always be mindful of the impact we have on everyone and everything and expect the best for ourselves and others. Blessings!!

Table of Contents

"*Everything is energy.*
Match the frequency of
the reality you want and
you cannot help but get
that reality.
It can be no other way.
This is not philosophy.
This is physics."
~*Albert Einstein*

Vibrations - The Keys to Success or Failure, to Wealth or Poverty, to Health or Dis-ease

Everything is "frequency." But what is frequency? In essence, frequency is the rate of vibration and oscillation measured over a specific period of time (usually one second). In layman's terms, it's simply a repeating sequence. Take a heartbeat, for example – the average heart rate frequency is 60-100 beats per minute. The basis of every state of mind and matter, including conditions of disease or health, is the primary state of the vibration.

The food we eat, the air we breathe, the words we speak and the ecological systems in which we live influence the switches that turn on and off the expression of our genes and DNA. Additionally, the signals generated from our perceptions of the world we live in, our thoughts, beliefs, prayers, meditations and intentions influence our inner environment, cause chemical changes in our body and brain, and affect the way our genes communicate instructions to our cells and literally have the effect of altering and activating our DNA.

Everything vibrates with an energy; the higher the energy, the higher the frequency. Positive feelings and thoughts evoke a higher frequency vs. negative feelings and thoughts which evoke a lower frequency. Real food that has been grown and had life has higher frequency than not-foods that come in a box, can, or bag and have never had life and therefore have zero frequency. Everything you put into your body, your mind, your soul – is raising or lowering your personal frequency, which will determine your health (or lack of it), your success (or lack of it), etc. The frequency of a healthy human body is usually between 62-78 Hz.

Your entire existence...all matter, all life, all experiences–everything owes its existence in the physical world to frequency. Absolutely everything is frequency. You cannot have an experience on this planet without attracting it through frequency. Every emotion, including love and hate, tunes into a specific frequency. Health has a frequency. Disease has frequency. Success has a frequency. Failure has a frequency. Your organs are each tuned to a specific frequency, as is your entire body which resonates at its own frequency.

You are a symphony of frequencies while you project yourself through this universe and create your physical reality. You are a master of your energy, and thus you are able to control everything you are, everything you do, everything you experience. From the day you are born until the day you die nothing will ever change the fact that you are both a frequency emitter and receiver in flux with your internal and external environment.

Our energy is blocked when we experience negativity, fear, and even unhealthy substances. Think about this...When you consume really unhealthy food, alcohol, or drugs, doesn't your energy feel low, or dull or blocked? Low vibrations mean a dampened energy field. It also means a disconnection to other things, the universe, and ourselves. Plus, a constant negative, low vibration/frequency state can lead to sickness and disease in the body.

Chronic disease occurs when voltage drops below a certain level. Cells then don't have enough energy to work correctly and the amount of oxygen in the cells drops, switching from aerobic (oxygen-available) metabolism to anaerobic (oxygen-diminished) metabolism. If the frequency drops to 58 Hz, cold and flu symptoms can appear, at 55 Hz diseases like Candida can take hold, at 52 Hz Epstein Barre, and at 42 Hz Cancer.

Well, our thoughts {much like our feelings} also produce vibrations and our vibrations are like a magnet. So, if we are thinking positive thoughts, feeling good and operating at a high vibrational frequency, we are going to attract experiences and people that match this frequency. But, if we are thinking negative thoughts and are down on ourselves or the world, we are going to put that out there in the universe and attract it right back.

We Are The Masters Of Our Own Destiny

Did you know that success, abundance, wealth, health, happiness - all of them have certain vibrations that can be voluntarily produced by your thoughts and emotions?

The universe is impartial – it doesn't judge or decide who should be punished. It simply responds to what we give out and express. Sometimes we fall into a victim mindset, believing that we are chronically unlucky, predisposed to bad health, or working through some accumulated karma. Mostly, however, we are simply dealing with the experiences, situations, and people that we're attracting, like a magnet, through our own personal frequency. Thankfully, through mindfulness and strong intention, we have the power to bring into our lives positivity, health, wealth, happiness, success, etc.

Epigenetic Therapy, correctly practiced, is potentially the most significant breakthrough in the fields of health and longevity to date. This approach allows us to address a predisposition to certain states of health and being. Raising one's vibration, as a conscious focus, can do much to alleviate conditions that one was predisposed to manifest in physical form. The applied practice of this new awareness is empowering, for we can learn to become masters of our destiny instead of victims of our genes.

Physician and best-selling author Deepak Chopra teaches us that we can actually modify our own genes and initiate DNA activation through our actions and behaviors. Miraculous healing occurs as a result of shifts in the consciousness of belief, intention, spiritual practice and prayer.

There is a scale of vibrations, and we can consciously decide to raise our vibrations. Start thinking in a positive way. Make your thoughts pure and improve your life by restructuring your paradigm, also known as your conditioned mind - your subconscious beliefs and thoughts that represent your core vibration.

The moment you start entertaining thoughts of love, compassion, bliss, kindness, gratefulness, confidence, abundance, health - you instantly raise your vibrations. Turn this into a habit - and you're a completely new person!

On the other side, all negative emotions such as fear, doubt, worry, jealousy, resentment, guilt, anger, and the like - they lower your levels of vibrations and you "break windows" wherever you go. You are literally attracted to everything that has a corresponding frequency of vibration, and trust me-- you're not going to enjoy the things that will come in to your life!

You can even feel it... Listen to some highly successful individual talk about the way he or she is thinking. Watch some of their interviews, watch how they walk, observe and try to feel the aura their entire being is producing. You can feel their success, confidence and self-respect.

Then do the same with a less successful individual, or observe a sick person... There's a sickness in the air that you can feel even without them doing any talking at all.

Every cell in your body resonates with your thoughts, feelings, and words. Every thought you have, every emotion you feel, every word you speak is feeding either health or dis-ease, success or failure, life or death. There is no middle ground. Take captive every thought, before it becomes a feeling or a word. Is it offering life, health, success, happiness? If not, trade it for one that is. Additionally, the signals generated from our *perceptions* of the world we live in cause chemical changes in our body and brain and affect the way our genes communicate instructions to our cells and literally have the effect of altering and activating DNA.

Epigenetics shows us that through conscious intention we can change our quality of life from what we have been handed down from previous generations. The science confirms that it is our individual choices, based on our degree of consciousness, that play a role and change our cellular structure and level of DNA activation. The research behind the science encourages us to abandon obsolete beliefs that we are victims of predetermined genetic codes and circumstances. Epigenetics clarifies how perceptions of our inner and outer environments shape our biology and behavior and make us masters of our own lives, rewriting the rules of disease, heredity, and well-being.

As human beings, we actually choose our experiences by the way we resonate or vibrate as an energy field. How can ten people experience the same situation and choose completely different responses, thus obtaining completely different outcomes? *Perception.*

Speak the language the Universe speaks - energetic vibration. The energy of your thoughts creates your reality. So, become conscious of your thoughts. Everything you think, say, and feel becomes your reality. If you have a negative thought just tell it to go away. It's that easy. You have complete control over your thoughts. You get to choose. No one else chooses your thoughts for you, so take responsibility for them. The lower your vibration, the more likely you are to attract circumstances to you that mirror this, and the higher your vibration, the more good you will attract and doors will open to all the positive healthy stuff!

*Everything you think,
say, and feel
becomes your reality.*

Create Your Reality

First thing every morning when you wake up, start declaring God's blessings and favor over your life. Pronounce and affirm positive things you wish to give birth to in your life with energy and expectation. Remember that the words you speak are seeds of power that set in motion the destiny you will inherit. Take captive every thought throughout the day to make sure nothing you think or say contradicts your amazing future!

Choose to speak powerful words of life. No corrupt communication shall proceed out of my mouth (Eph. 4:29). I boldly declare the positive things I desire to happen with absolute faith and authority (Matt 17:20). I exhale encouraging words of inspiration into the lives of those around me (Heb 3:13).

We have the power within us to create. The words we speak sow the seeds of our future. Speaking declarations that align with God's truth bring our mind, body, and spirit into agreement. If we want to walk in the fullness of His blessing, we must constantly confess words full of life and victory.

What we verbalize is a direct reflection of the beliefs we have internalized. The way we choose to express ourselves verbally dictates what we attract into our lives. We have the ability to bless, curse, heal, or destroy every time we utter something out of our mouths. Acknowledging this transformative power is essential to building a life of success.

Words set outcomes into motion; therefore, it's vital for us to think before we speak. We must stay disciplined, keeping watch over our mouth at all times. When we learn to tame our tongue, we take control of our destiny.

Success has to be first spoken into existence. Each word we speak is either carrying us closer to or further away from our goals and dreams. Whether we are encouraging a friend, launching a new business, or leading an organization, every verbal expression sends out a wave of energy impacting the environment around us. The things we say, when applied with the other natural laws, have the power to change the world.

Stop making excuses and just go do what it takes to get the things you want in life.

Set the tone for the day by establishing a morning routine of power and purpose. (take ownership)

Stay charged up by eating, drinking, and sleeping healthy and exercising regularly.

7 Ways To Raise Your Vibration

1. Become conscious of your thoughts. Everything you think, say or feel becomes your reality. Every single thought that comes into your head has an impact on you. For example, I spent a period of time when I was overwhelmed telling myself "I can't get up on time and exercise in the morning, I am just too tired, even though I have slept 7-8 hours." I struggled with this for months, feeling more and more tired, getting out of shape, losing my focus, and finally realized I had allowed the overwhelm to take over. This was during the time I had stopped my morning and evening practice of aligning my thoughts and setting my intentions. I began waking up and telling myself that my body needs exercise to stay healthy, that sedentary lifestyle is a number one killer, and I love the way I feel when I'm taking time for regular exercise. When you change those thoughts for the positive, your reality is likely to become positive too. Easier said than done in the face of adversity though, right? How about this, the next time a negative thought shows up in your head, take the time to acknowledge it, thank it for showing up, and then dismiss it and turn it around for the positive.

2. Be conscious of the foods you eat. REAL foods vibrate at high frequencies, and non-foods have a very low frequency (i.e., broccoli has a high vibration, as do blueberries; Big Macs and French fries don't vibrate at all). If you are consuming foods covered in chemicals and pesticides, or foods found within plastic or boxed packaging, cans, genetically-modified foods, it will leave you vibrating lower. Conversely, consume good quality organic produce, food as nature intended it, REAL food that has actually sustained life (high vibration/frequency), raw nuts and seeds, berries, and feel the high vibrations disseminate throughout your body. Most importantly, pay attention to how eating certain foods make you feel. The food you eat has influence on your thoughts and emotions. Food can be your catalyst to greater health and higher levels of vibrations, but it can also be the destroyer that has exactly the opposite effect. Everything you eat is either offering you health or dis-ease, life or death. There is no middle ground.

3. Drink water. Always ensure you drink plenty of water (purified or filtered is best) to assist your body to flush out toxicity day to day. Toxicity has a marked impact on our vibration so we must do what we can to reduce its impact within us and around us. The body requires half your weight in ounces daily to function properly. Any caffeine or alcohol intake must be compensated with more water.

4. Meditate. Sit in a comfortable position, close your eyes, and breath in and out. Too often we rush through our days with a scattered brain, leaving us in a state of anxiety and stress. Meditation helps to calm your spirit down and put you in a peaceful state of mind. Just 10 minutes of meditation a day can change your life forever.

5. Be grateful. Making a gratitude list shifts your vibrations from focusing on what you don't have to what is already abundant in your life. There is more to be grateful for than you could possibly imagine. For example, every morning when I wake up, I write down 3 things that I am grateful for that day. This is the beginning of becoming intentional, taking control of your thoughts, raising your frequency, and experiencing life on a higher level.

6. Practice acts of kindness. Giving to someone else (without expecting anything in return) shifts your thinking from "I don't have enough" or "Woe is me", to "I have more than enough to give to others." Abundance is a high vibration. In the same vein, being kind (as opposed to being mean) puts you at a high vibration. When you gossip or treat others badly, your vibration will suffer.

7. Get your blood pumping. Vibration requires movement, the more you move the better your vibrations move. So, Get Active! Dance! The happier you feel, the more you will draw happy experiences to yourself because you are operating at a different frequency.

"Success is nothing more than a few simple disciplines, practiced every day."

~JIM ROHN~

ATTITUDE OF GRATITUDE

What are three things that you can be grateful today?

One of the greatest gifts we have is the ability to choose what to focus on. An attitude of gratitude can completely transform your life and is the surest pathway to both success and happiness. It changes perspective. It can sweep away the petty day-to-day annoyances that bring up feelings of impatience, intolerance, negative judgment, indignation, anger, resentment, self-pity. Negative feelings actually lower your vibrational frequency and leave you attracting more negativity and things of low energy, keeping you unable to attract healthier things.

Gratitude is an experience of counting one's blessings, directing your thoughts. No matter where you are and what your situation is, your focus can be shifted to something positive, which raises your vibrational frequency.

Gratitude can transform your life on every level ~ mind/body/spirit.

Here are some ideas to get you going:

I am grateful for....

1. *My body's ability to heal itself when I give it what it needs*

2. *Having a supportive and loving family*

3. *The ability to walk and use my hands*

Another little secret: You can write things you are grateful for that you may not yet have in your life. For example, if you desire a different career you can write....*I am grateful to have the career of my dreams* (making sure to visualize details about that career).

A 2003 study by Emmons and McCullough found that keeping a daily gratitude journal leads to better sleep, reduction in physical pain, a greater sense of well-being, and a better ability to handle change.

Paul Mills, a Professor of Family Medicine and Public Health at the University of California San Diego School of Medicine, conducted studies that looked at the role of gratitude on heart health. Among other things, he found that participants who kept a journal writing 2-3 things they were grateful for every day had reduced levels of inflammation and improved heart rhythm compared to people who did not. He also found they showed a decreased risk of heart disease after only 2 months of this routine!

Dan Mager writes in *Psychology Today* that "Gratitude facilitates contentment, promotes physical health, enhances sleep, strengthens relationships, and encourages 'paying it forward'."

EMPOWERED BELIEFS

What empowered belief will I adopt to replace a limiting belief that has held me back?

As Tony Robbins, the nation's #1 Life and Business Strategist, says: "Beliefs have the power to create and the power to destroy. Human beings have the awesome ability to take any experience of their lives and create a meaning that disempowers them or one that can literally save their lives."

There is a vibrational pattern attached to each belief we hold. By releasing limiting beliefs that are low frequency and choosing high frequency beliefs that are of Heart Consciousness, we create frequencies that affect our bodies, our DNA, and enhance our ability to create a reality we choose to live within. What is really amazing is that we can easily create an illness or enjoy vitality just by becoming aware of our environments, perceptions, beliefs, thoughts, and intentions. Our consciously formed beliefs, thoughts, prayers and intentions have a much stronger effect on our lives than our genes do.

Limiting beliefs have more of a negative impact on your life than any other factor. They constrain us and impoverish our lives. The great news is that the choice is completely yours. You can eliminate limiting beliefs and replace them with beliefs that empower you.

Changing limiting beliefs to empowered beliefs can transform your life on every level ~ mind/body/spirit.

Success has to be first spoken into existence. Each word we speak, thought we think, is either moving us closer to or further away from our goals and dreams. Whether we are encouraging a friend, starting a new weight loss/work out program, launching a new business, dealing with a health issue, or leading an organization, every belief sends out a wave of energy that impacts us and the environment around us. The things we say, when applied to the other natural laws, have the power to change the world.

Identify the beliefs that are holding you back. Seven examples of limiting beliefs:
- I can't be my real self or I'll be judged.
- I could never attract the kind of spouse I want.
- I can't ask for what I want because I may get rejected.
- I can't pursue my dreams because I may fail.
- I am broke and can't afford....
- I could never do that....
- It's too hard to eat and live healthy.

What empowered belief will I adopt to replace a limiting belief...

I have what it takes to be successful and independent.

Stop believing and accepting the lies and settling for less than what you want. All negative mindsets, thoughts, and feelings create low frequency that every cell in your body obeys and you create a negative/low-frequency energy that attracts same. The energy of your beliefs creates your reality. When your beliefs change, your life will also change. Create beliefs that will improve your life, health, relationships, career, finances. Raise your vibrational frequency to attract things of higher frequency (good health, success, healthy relationships, happiness).

HEALTHY CHANGES

(Foundations of Health Include: hydration, nutrition, respiration, restoration, recreation, emotional wellness, spiritual wellness)

What healthy choice(s) would make today really great?

Improving your health - mind/body/spirit - requires effort, willpower, and a real commitment to make long-term changes. You don't have to do it all at once, and an occasional lapse doesn't mean you can't start again. Every change becomes easier as it becomes more firmly incorporated into your familiar routine. Keeping the body healthy physically, mentally/emotionally, and spiritually raises our vibrational frequency so that we can attract those things of higher frequency.

Making healthy choices can transform your life on every level - mind/body/spirit.

1. The human body needs half its weight in ounces of purified (clean, filtered) water every day to assist your body in flushing out toxicity. Toxicity has a marked impact on our vibration, so we must do what we can to reduce its impact while staying adequately hydrated for optimal body functions. Dehydration lowers your vibrational frequency and leads to chronic toxicity, disease, mental/physical/emotional imbalances, and much more. Caffeine, alcohol and sugary drinks do nothing to hydrate the body but cause dehydration and lower the vibrational frequency.

Here are seven important reasons to drink half your weight in ounces of purified water daily:

- Increases energy and relieves fatigue
- Helps flush toxins from the body
- Improves your mental abilities
- Prevents sore joints
- Prevent headaches
- Helps you lose weight
- Makes your skin glow

2. Become conscious of the foods you eat. Real whole foods vibrate at high frequencies (organic fruits and vegetables, raw nuts and seeds, etc.) while processed, packaged, and fast foods are very low frequency (Big Macs and fries don't vibrate at all). If you are consuming foods covered in chemicals and pesticides, foods found within plastic or boxed packaging, cans, it will create a low frequency environment within you. Alternately, consuming good quality organic produce, food as nature intended it, you will feel the high frequencies disseminate throughout your body. Everything we needed was given to us in the garden. It is important to pay attention to how eating certain foods make your body feel.

Seven important reasons to eat clean, real food:

- Reduce your risk for chronic diseases
- Boost your immune system
- Maintain strong bones and muscles
- Maintain a healthy weight
- Reverse chronic ailments
- Boost energy
- Slow down the aging process

3. It has been found that over 50% of adults are chest breathers, which contributes to a number of problems like rapid heartbeats, low oxygen levels, toxicity, and depression. We need to aim for diaphragmatic (belly) breathing as often as we can (10 deep breaths upon waking, after lunch, and before sleep is a great start).

Deep breathing benefits health mind/body/spirit in these seven ways:
- Helps alleviate stress, improving confidence
- Helps create better circulation and oxygenation, which also enhances metabolism and greater energy
- Assists with detoxification, up to 3 lbs per week of toxin release with daily practice
- Improves digestion and the health of all organ systems
- Improves posture, heart health, and sleep
- Pain relief
- Regulates weight

4. Being asleep may seem like the ultimate form of inactivity, but those unconscious hours are actually a time of hard work for your body. "Sleeping is one way that your body recovers from damage and protects itself against illness", says Michael Twery, PhD, director of the National Center on Sleep Disorders Research for the National Heart Lung and Blood Institute. "Sleep is one part of the whole rhythm of life," Twery says. "Whenever researchers go in and disrupt that rhythm, the biology becomes less efficient, and that inefficiency basically leads to disease." Adequate sleep raises your vibrational frequency and is vital for good health and success.

A WebMD article from October 6, 2016, "The Healing Power of Sleep" lists these seven benefits:
- Saves you hundreds of calories
- Makes you smarter
- Brightens your mood
- Heals you from the inside out
- Guards your heart
- Revs you up
- Makes tough decisions easier

5. The human body was designed for 'movement.' John Hopkins University, the WHO (World Health Organization) and MedLinePlus.gov, to name just a few, warn that sedentary lifestyle can be the cause of many chronic diseases and may also lead to premature death, also contributing to anxiety and depression. The human body needs up to 30 minutes every day of some form of physical activity (I like to call it "Fun Sweaty Activity", as it needs to be something you enjoy that can also work up a good sweat and move toxins out of the body, while increasing oxygenation and producing endorphins in the brain, which reduce pain perception and increase positive feelings, which also raises the vibrational frequency in the body).

The Mayo Clinic lists these seven ways exercise can lead to a happier, healthier you:
- Controls weight
- Combats health conditions and diseases
- Improves mood
- Boosts energy
- Promotes better sleep
- Puts the spark back into your sex life
- It can be fun....and social

6. Emotional Wellness is an important part of overall health. People who are emotionally healthy are in control of their thoughts, feelings, and behaviors. They are able to cope with life's challenges. They can keep problems in perspective and bounce back from setbacks. They feel good about themselves and have good relationships. Research shows that emotional health is a skill. It allows you to realize your full potential. You can work productively and cope with the stresses of everyday life. It helps you work with other people and contribute to society.

It also affects your physical health. Research shows a link between an upbeat mental state and physical signs of good health. These include lower blood pressure, reduced risk of heart disease, and a healthier weight.

Seven really great natural, easy ways to foster emotional wellness include:
- Love (for yourself and for others)
- Practicing acts of kindness
- Laughter therapy
- Sound therapy
- Aromatherapy
- Stress reduction
- Releasing trapped emotions (emotional freedom technique, tapping, flower essence therapy, etc)

7. Spiritual Wellness (Prayer/Meditation)
Prayer is a very personal experience that can mean something different to each of us. At least 55 percent of people in the United States pray every day, and many more pray once per week or month. Research shows that prayer significantly benefits our emotional, physical, and mental health.

It is important to sincerely find prayer meaningful in your life. If you're only doing it out of a feeling of obligation or for personal gain, research shows it can actually have a detrimental effect. Whereas, prayer, meditation, or other spiritual practices that maintain a focus outside of yourself have the most benefits.

Here are seven proven health benefits of prayer:
1. Improves self-control
Scientists refer to the "strength model" of self-control, which suggests our cognitive resources, like our physical resources, have a limited strength. Most of us have likely experienced this. By the end of a long day, sometimes you simply don't have the mental energy to go for a run or make healthy food choices.

A German study found that prayer can counteract this mental fatigue and boost your self-control. Those who had prayed briefly prior to a mentally demanding task were able to complete a challenging test afterwards without showing any cognitive depletion. Those who had not prayed prior to the task did not perform as well on the test.

Researchers at Queen's University had similar findings. Over four separate experiments, participants exercised greater self-control when subtle reminders of religious concepts were present.

2. Enhances Relationships
Prayer can have a significant impact on your close relationships. Studies have shown that praying for a friend or intimate partner can increase your forgiveness towards them, as well as foster greater trust in the relationship. It's also been found that those who pray for their romantic partners commit less infidelity.

In addition, one study looked at how people felt about the sacrifices they made in their close relationships. This is often a good indicator of your overall satisfaction with the relationship. The study found that praying for someone you're close to increases your satisfaction with making sacrifices for your relationship. This helped people resolve disagreements more effectively and feel closer and more understood by their partner.

3. Improves Ability To Cope With Stress

A University of Florida study discovered that 96 percent of older adults specifically use prayer to cope with stress. In fact, prayer was the most frequently reported alternative treatment seniors use to feel better and maintain health in general. One-third of the respondents also reported using other spiritual strategies to improve their health, including imagery, music, art therapy, energy healing, humor, meditation and religious counseling. Seniors who prayed or used any other spiritual techniques were also found to have more positive and self-reliant coping strategies.

4. Turns On "Disease-Fighting" Genes

Researchers at Harvard Medical School discovered that relaxation techniques, including yoga, meditation, and repetitive prayer and mantra, are able to activate numerous "disease-fighting" genes in your body. Relaxation practices appear to switch on genes that protect you from various disorders, such as high blood pressure, cancer, infertility and rheumatoid arthritis. The more regularly you practice a relaxation technique, the more benefit you'll receive.

5. Combats Depression

Prayer has been shown to improve our overall sense of well-being. This may be due to the fact that prayer, meditation, and other spiritual practices can increase your dopamine levels. Dopamine is a neurotransmitter that's released when you feel pleasure and happiness. It enhances your positive emotions, motivation, and cognitive abilities. Healthy dopamine levels are also known to prevent depression and anxiety.

Another study investigated adults at high risk for depression, based on family history. Typically, people at high risk have been shown to have thinning in certain regions of their brain cortex. Brain scans on those who placed a high importance on religion or spirituality showed significantly thicker cortices in exactly the same regions that showed thinning in those who were nonspiritual. And people who included spirituality in their lives had 90 percent less risk of developing major depression.

6. Helps Control Pain
A Bowling Green State University study found that spiritual meditation or prayer helped reduce the number of headaches practitioners experience. Researchers asked people who suffer from migraines to meditate for 20 minutes each day by repeating a spiritual mantra, such as "God is good. God is peace. God is love." A second group was asked to use a nonspiritual mantra, such as "Grass is green. Sand is soft." After a month, those who had used a spiritual mantra had less headaches and greater pain tolerance. Whereas, the neutral mantra appeared to have no benefit.

7. Promotes Longer Life
A survey published in the JOURNAL OF GERONTOLOGY polled 4,000 senior citizens and found that those who prayed or meditated regularly coped better with illness and lived longer than those who did not. These results are likely due to a combination of all the other proven benefits of prayer that boost your overall mental and physical health.

What healthy choice(s) would make today really great?

I am going to eat a salad for lunch today and laugh out loud three times

DAILY AFFIRMATION

A statement of what you want for your life

A Daily Affirmation is a simple statement that defines you as you want to be. Every time you write the Daily Affirmation, you prime your brain to start building this belief in your mind. With consistency, you will begin to create that change within.

Affirmations put you in the driver's seat of your mind and flood it with positive information that can completely transform your life, mind/body/spirit.

There is MRI evidence suggesting that certain neural pathways are increased when people practice self-affirmations (Cascio et al., 2016). Empirical studies suggest that positive self-affirmation practices can: decrease health-deteriorating stress, increase physical activity, makes us less likely to dismiss harmful health messages and respond instead with intention to change for the better, assist in academic achievement, and make us more resilient to difficulties when they come.

Daily affirmations can transform your life on every level - mind/body/spirit.

They could look something like these:

Daily Affirmations. I am....

I am an amazing, confident, successful woman.
I am an overcomer and can write my own story.
I am powerful and impact the world positively.

Here are seven examples of Affirmations:

- I live with passion and purpose.
- I am confident and comfortable in my own skin.
- I am healthy and full of energy.
- I am resilient, strong, brave, and can't be destroyed.
- I deserve to earn the money I am worth.
- I am too big a gift to the world to waste my time on self-pity and sadness.
- I am creative and resourceful.

BEFORE GOING TO SLEEP:

THE AMAZING THREE

What are three amazing things that happened today?

Taking inventory of all the positive moments – big and small – will allow your thoughts to begin shifting from bad habits of complaining or making excuses and will raise your vibrational frequency. You will be able to track your growth and progress over the months.

When you write your Amazing Three, you count your blessings in the day, which has the effect of priming your brain and can transform not only relationships with loved ones, it can also transform your relationship with yourself, your job, the world.

Identifying amazing things that happen to you can transform your life – mind/body/spirit.

Start with something simple for the first few weeks:

Three amazing things that happened today...

1. *I went to the park and walked during my lunch break today.*

2. *I finally thought of an idea for my new project at work.*

3. *I talked with an old friend and had a great conversation.*

With consistency, your list will start getting more and more amazing. Review your Amazing Three every month to see how your life is transforming on every level - mind/body/spirit.

MAKING THE DAY BETTER

What could I have done to make today even better?

This section is your personal reminder that you have the power to change your perception of the past and influence your future. Your perception shapes your reality. As we have already established, priming your brain to automatically scan for positives upon waking every morning is a very effective and powerful way to begin the day. However, chances are your automatic responses will kick in during the day while you are developing these new skills.

Frustrations with a family member or attending a work event full of junk food when you are trying to make healthy changes for yourself are pretty common problems. At the end of the day you get to update your perception of the actions you took and begin to look at ways that you could have done something different to make your day even better.

Think of this as an imagination exercise where you get the chance to go back in time and change one thing you did during the day. It could be waking up earlier. It could be trusting your gut with a decision. For example, if you felt bad about how you responded to a family member you could write:

How could I have made today even better?

I practiced deep breathing and kindness for my family member rather than hurting them with my impatience and frustration.

As you begin building a pattern of looking at problems and the actions you can take to move through them, your perception will begin to shift and you will experience healthy transformations on every level – mind/body/spirit.

VISUALIZE YOUR SUCCESS

What would make tomorrow really great?

"*Never go to sleep without a request to your subconscious.*"
~Thomas Edison

This is the perfect time to reflect on your goals and intentions, visualizing your goals coming true. Tap into the feeling you have at this moment and feel it in the present. The things you focus on will begin to show up in your life.

There is a small part of your brain called the Reticular Activation System (RAS) that turns on and off your perception of ideas and thoughts and determines the lenses through which you look at the world. When you write "What would make tomorrow really great?" you are taking a step to influence your RAS to point out and engage in activities that would make your day really great. You are building new pathways in your brain that allow you to 'see' what to do to improve your well-being every day.

Here's an example:

What would make tomorrow really great?

Taking extra time for myself before going to work (to walk, meditate, etc.).

Be sure to write down what you have control over, focusing on specific actions that you can take in the day to make it really great. This will create a new program in your mind that will naturally raise your vibrational frequency and bring about amazing transformations in your life on every level – mind/body/spirit.

Date ___/___/20___

"Choice, not chance, determines human destiny." ~Anonymous

I am grateful for....

1._____
2._____
3._____

What empowered belief will I adopt to replace a limiting belief that has held me back?

_____

What healthy choice would make today really great?

_____

Daily Affirmations. I am....

_____
_____
_____

3 Amazing things that happened today...

1._____
2._____
3._____

How could I have made today even better?

_____

What would make tomorrow really great?

_____
_____

Date ___/___/20___

"We are what we repeatedly do. Excellence then is not an act, but a habit." ~ Aristotle

I am grateful for....

1._____
2._____
3._____

What empowered belief will I adopt to replace a limiting belief that has held me back?

_____

What healthy choice would make today really great?

_____

Daily Affirmations. I am....

_____
_____
_____

3 Amazing things that happened today...

1._____
2._____
3._____

How could I have made today even better?

_____

What would make tomorrow really great?

_____

Date ___/___/20___

"If you keep on living like the way you are now, you will continue to produce the same life you already have." ~ Jim Rohn

I am grateful for....

1._____
2._____
3._____

What empowered belief will I adopt to replace a limiting belief that has held me back?

_____

What healthy choice would make today really great?

_____

Daily Affirmations. I am....

_____
_____
_____

3 Amazing things that happened today...

1._____
2._____
3._____

How could I have made today even better?

_____

What would make tomorrow really great?

_____
_____

Date ___/___/20___

"One will never get more than he thinks he can get." ~ Bruce Lee

I am grateful for....

1._____
2._____
3._____

What empowered belief will I adopt to replace a limiting belief that has held me back?

_____

What healthy choice would make today really great?

_____

Daily Affirmations. I am....

_____
_____

3 Amazing things that happened today...

1._____
2._____
3._____

How could I have made today even better?

_____

What would make tomorrow really great?

_____

Date ___/___/20___

"You have to expect things of yourself before you can do them." ~
Michael Jordan

I am grateful for....

1._____
2._____
3._____

What empowered belief will I adopt to replace a limiting belief
that has held me back?

_____

What healthy choice would make today really great?

_____

Daily Affirmations. I am....

_____
_____

3 Amazing things that happened today...

1._____
2._____
3._____

How could I have made today even better?

_____

What would make tomorrow really great?

_____

Date ___/___/20___

"Every cell in your body is eavesdropping on your thoughts."
~ Deepak Chopra

I am grateful for....

1._____
2._____
3._____

What empowered belief will I adopt to replace a limiting belief
that has held me back?

_____

What healthy choice would make today really great?

_____

Daily Affirmations. I am....

_____
_____
_____

3 Amazing things that happened today...

1._____
2._____
3._____

How could I have made today even better?

_____

What would make tomorrow really great?

_____
_____

Date ___/___/20___

"Smile and laugh at all mealtimes for healthier digestion and elimination." ~Dr. N.W. Walker

I am grateful for....

1._____
2._____
3._____

What empowered belief will I adopt to replace a limiting belief that has held me back?

_____

What healthy choice would make today really great?

_____

Daily Affirmations. I am....

_____
_____
_____

3 Amazing things that happened today...

1._____
2._____
3._____

How could I have made today even better?

_____

What would make tomorrow really great?

_____
_____

Date ___/___/20___

"It was character that got us out of bed, commitment that moves us into action, and discipline that enabled us to follow through." ~ Zig Ziggler

I am grateful for....

1._____
2._____
3._____

What empowered belief will I adopt to replace a limiting belief that has held me back?

_____

What healthy choice would make today really great?

_____

Daily Affirmations. I am....

_____
_____
_____

3 Amazing things that happened today...

1._____
2._____
3._____

How could I have made today even better?

_____

What would make tomorrow really great?

_____
_____

Date ___/___/20___

"In reading the lives of great men, I found that the first victory they won was over themselves." ~ Harry S. Truman

I am grateful for....

1._____
2._____
3._____

What empowered belief will I adopt to replace a limiting belief that has held me back?

_____

What healthy choice would make today really great?

_____

Daily Affirmations. I am....

_____
_____
_____

3 Amazing things that happened today...

1._____
2._____
3._____

How could I have made today even better?

_____

What would make tomorrow really great?

_____

Date ___/___/20___

"Death and life are in the power of the tongue: and they that love it shall eat the fruit thereof." ~Proverbs 18:21

I am grateful for....

1._____
2._____
3._____

What empowered belief will I adopt to replace a limiting belief that has held me back?

_____

What healthy choice would make today really great?

_____

Daily Affirmations. I am....

_____
_____

3 Amazing things that happened today...

1._____
2._____
3._____

How could I have made today even better?

_____

What would make tomorrow really great?

_____

Date ___/___/20___

"One day you shall reap what you have sown, so make sure you are planting the type of seeds you want to see grow in your future." ~
Billy Alsbrook

I am grateful for....

1._____
2._____
3._____

What empowered belief will I adopt to replace a limiting belief that has held me back?

_____

What healthy choice would make today really great?

_____

Daily Affirmations. I am....

_____
_____

3 Amazing things that happened today...

1._____
2._____
3._____

How could I have made today even better?

_____

What would make tomorrow really great?

_____

Date ___/___/20___

"Self-discipline begins with the mastery of your thoughts. If you don't control what you think, you can't control what you do."
~ Napolean Hill

I am grateful for....

1._____
2._____
3._____

What empowered belief will I adopt to replace a limiting belief that has held me back?

_____

What healthy choice would make today really great?

_____

Daily Affirmations. I am....

_____
_____

3 Amazing things that happened today...

1._____
2._____
3._____

How could I have made today even better?

_____

What would make tomorrow really great?

_____

Date ___/___/20___

"Give me six hours to cut down a tree, and I will spend the first four sharpening my blade." ~ Abraham Lincoln

I am grateful for....

1._____
2._____
3._____

What empowered belief will I adopt to replace a limiting belief that has held me back?

_____

What healthy choice would make today really great?

_____

Daily Affirmations. I am....

_____
_____
_____

3 Amazing things that happened today...

1._____
2._____
3._____

How could I have made today even better?

_____

What would make tomorrow really great?

_____
_____

Date ___/___/20___

"When you realize the awesome power of words, you can change lives." ~ Tammy Kling

I am grateful for....

1._____
2._____
3._____

What empowered belief will I adopt to replace a limiting belief that has held me back?

_____

What healthy choice would make today really great?

_____

Daily Affirmations. I am....

_____
_____
_____

3 Amazing things that happened today...

1._____
2._____
3._____

How could I have made today even better?

_____

What would make tomorrow really great?

_____
_____

Date ___/___/20___

I am grateful for....

1._____
2._____
3._____

What empowered belief will I adopt to replace a limiting belief that has held me back?

_____

What healthy choice would make today really great?

_____

Daily Affirmations. I am....

_____
_____
_____

3 Amazing things that happened today...

1._____
2._____
3._____

How could I have made today even better?

_____

What would make tomorrow really great?

_____
_____

Date ___/___/20___

"Most people knock on the door of their dreams once, then run away before anyone has a chance to open the door. But if you keep knocking, persistently and endlessly, eventually the door will open." ~ Les Brown

I am grateful for....

1._____
2._____
3._____

What empowered belief will I adopt to replace a limiting belief that has held me back?

_____

What healthy choice would make today really great?

_____

Daily Affirmations. I am....

_____
_____

3 Amazing things that happened today...

1._____
2._____
3._____

How could I have made today even better?

_____

What would make tomorrow really great?

_____
_____

Date ___ /___ /20___

"If you always let others think for you, you'll never become who you want to be." ~ Mission.org

I am grateful for....

1._____
2._____
3._____

What empowered belief will I adopt to replace a limiting belief that has held me back?

_____

What healthy choice would make today really great?

_____

Daily Affirmations. I am....

_____
_____
_____

3 Amazing things that happened today...

1._____
2._____
3._____

How could I have made today even better?

_____

What would make tomorrow really great?

_____
_____

Date ___/___/20___

"When our true self doesn't get a chance to follow its desires, it acts out in strange ways." ~ David Kadavy

I am grateful for....

1._____
2._____
3._____

What empowered belief will I adopt to replace a limiting belief that has held me back?

_____

What healthy choice would make today really great?

_____

Daily Affirmations. I am....

_____
_____
_____

3 Amazing things that happened today...

1._____
2._____
3._____

How could I have made today even better?

_____

What would make tomorrow really great?

_____
_____

Date ___/___/20___

"It's a funny thing about life; once you begin to take note of the things you are grateful for you begin to lose sight of the things that you lack."

~ Germany Kent

I am grateful for....

1._____
2._____
3._____

What empowered belief will I adopt to replace a limiting belief that has held me back?

_____

What healthy choice would make today really great?

_____

Daily Affirmations. I am....

_____
_____
_____

3 Amazing things that happened today...

1._____
2._____
3._____

How could I have made today even better?

_____

What would make tomorrow really great?

_____
_____

Date ___/___/20___

"You were born an original, don't die a copy." ~ John Mason

I am grateful for....

1._____
2._____
3._____

What empowered belief will I adopt to replace a limiting belief that has held me back?

_____

What healthy choice would make today really great?

_____

Daily Affirmations. I am....

_____
_____
_____

3 Amazing things that happened today...

1._____
2._____
3._____

How could I have made today even better?

_____

What would make tomorrow really great?

_____
_____

Date ___/___/20___

"Belief, strong belief, triggers the mind to figure out ways and means how to." ~ Dr. David Schwartz

I am grateful for....

1._____
2._____
3._____

What empowered belief will I adopt to replace a limiting belief that has held me back?

_____

What healthy choice would make today really great?

_____

Daily Affirmations. I am....

_____
_____
_____

3 Amazing things that happened today...

1._____
2._____
3._____

How could I have made today even better?

_____

What would make tomorrow really great?

_____
_____

Date ___/___/20___

"Change your thoughts, and you change your world."
~ Norman Vincent Peale

I am grateful for....

1._____
2._____
3._____

What empowered belief will I adopt to replace a limiting belief that has held me back?

_____

What healthy choice would make today really great?

_____

Daily Affirmations. I am....

_____
_____
_____

3 Amazing things that happened today...

1._____
2._____
3._____

How could I have made today even better?

_____

What would make tomorrow really great?

_____
_____

Date ___/___/20___

"The words we choose to use when we communicate with each other, carry vibrations. The careful selection of words, helps to elevate our consciousness and resonate in higher frequencies." ~ Grigoris Deoudis

I am grateful for....

1._____
2._____
3._____

What empowered belief will I adopt to replace a limiting belief that has held me back?

_____

What healthy choice would make today really great?

_____

Daily Affirmations. I am....

_____

_____

3 Amazing things that happened today...

1._____
2._____
3._____

How could I have made today even better?

_____

What would make tomorrow really great?

_____

_____

Date ___/___/20___

"The part can never be well unless the whole is well." ~ Plato

I am grateful for....

1._____
2._____
3._____

What empowered belief will I adopt to replace a limiting belief that has held me back?

_____

What healthy choice would make today really great?

_____

Daily Affirmations. I am....

_____
_____
_____

3 Amazing things that happened today...

1._____
2._____
3._____

How could I have made today even better?

_____

What would make tomorrow really great?

_____
_____

Date ___/___/20___

"Physical fitness is not only one of the most important keys to a healthy body, it is the basis of dynamic and creative intellectual activity."

~ John F. Kennedy

I am grateful for....

1._____
2._____
3._____

What empowered belief will I adopt to replace a limiting belief that has held me back?

_____

What healthy choice would make today really great?

_____

Daily Affirmations. I am....

_____

_____

_____

3 Amazing things that happened today...

1._____
2._____
3._____

How could I have made today even better?

_____

What would make tomorrow really great?

_____

_____

Date ___/___/20___

"Change your words, change your life." ~ Tony Robbins

I am grateful for....

1._____
2._____
3._____

What empowered belief will I adopt to replace a limiting belief that has held me back?

_____

What healthy choice would make today really great?

_____

Daily Affirmations. I am....

_____
_____
_____

3 Amazing things that happened today...

1._____
2._____
3._____

How could I have made today even better?

_____

What would make tomorrow really great?

_____
_____

Date ___/___/20___

"Success comes to those who are success-conscious."
~ Napolean Hill

I am grateful for....

1._____
2._____
3._____

What empowered belief will I adopt to replace a limiting belief that has held me back?

_____

What healthy choice would make today really great?

_____

Daily Affirmations. I am....

_____
_____

3 Amazing things that happened today...

1._____
2._____
3._____

How could I have made today even better?

_____

What would make tomorrow really great?

_____
_____

Date ___/___/20___

"If you are not willing to risk the unusual, you will have to settle for the ordinary." ~ Jim Rohn

I am grateful for....

1._____
2._____
3._____

What empowered belief will I adopt to replace a limiting belief that has held me back?

_____

What healthy choice would make today really great?

_____

Daily Affirmations. I am....

_____
_____
_____

3 Amazing things that happened today...

1._____
2._____
3._____

How could I have made today even better?

_____

What would make tomorrow really great?

_____
_____

Date ___/___/20___

"Be willing to be a beginner every single morning."
~ Meister Eckhart

I am grateful for....

1._____
2._____
3._____

What empowered belief will I adopt to replace a limiting belief that has held me back?

_____

What healthy choice would make today really great?

_____

Daily Affirmations. I am....

_____
_____

3 Amazing things that happened today...

1._____
2._____
3._____

How could I have made today even better?

_____

What would make tomorrow really great?

_____
_____

Date ___/___/20___

"The secret of change is to focus all of your energy, not on fighting the old, but on building the new." ~ Socrates

I am grateful for....

1._____
2._____
3._____

What empowered belief will I adopt to replace a limiting belief that has held me back?

_____

What healthy choice would make today really great?

_____

Daily Affirmations. I am....

_____
_____
_____

3 Amazing things that happened today...

1._____
2._____
3._____

How could I have made today even better?

_____

What would make tomorrow really great?

_____
_____

Date ___/___/20___

"I am the master of my fate: I am the captain of my soul."
~ William Ernest Henley

I am grateful for....

1._____
2._____
3._____

What empowered belief will I adopt to replace a limiting belief that has held me back?

_____

What healthy choice would make today really great?

_____

Daily Affirmations. I am....

_____
_____

3 Amazing things that happened today...

1._____
2._____
3._____

How could I have made today even better?

_____

What would make tomorrow really great?

_____
_____

Date ___/___/20___

"Your actions reveal not what you want, but what you choose."
~ Shane Parrish

I am grateful for....

1._____
2._____
3._____

What empowered belief will I adopt to replace a limiting belief that has held me back?

_____

What healthy choice would make today really great?

_____

Daily Affirmations. I am....

_____
_____

3 Amazing things that happened today...

1._____
2._____
3._____

How could I have made today even better?

_____

What would make tomorrow really great?

_____

Date ___/___/20___

"No one can make you feel inferior without your permission."
~ Eleanor Roosevelt

I am grateful for....

1._____
2._____
3._____

What empowered belief will I adopt to replace a limiting belief that has held me back?

_____

What healthy choice would make today really great?

_____

Daily Affirmations. I am....

_____
_____

3 Amazing things that happened today...

1._____
2._____
3._____

How could I have made today even better?

_____

What would make tomorrow really great?

_____
_____

Date ___/___/20___

"Everyone wants to live on the top of the mountain, but all that happiness and growth occurs while you're climbing it."

~ Andy Rooney

I am grateful for....

1._____
2._____
3._____

What empowered belief will I adopt to replace a limiting belief that has held me back?

_____

What healthy choice would make today really great?

_____

Daily Affirmations. I am....

_____
_____
_____

3 Amazing things that happened today...

1._____
2._____
3._____

How could I have made today even better?

_____

What would make tomorrow really great?

_____
_____

Date ___/___/20___

"You cannot teach a man anything; you can only help him find it within himself." ~ Galileo

I am grateful for....

1._____
2._____
3._____

What empowered belief will I adopt to replace a limiting belief that has held me back?

_____

What healthy choice would make today really great?

_____

Daily Affirmations. I am....

_____
_____
_____

3 Amazing things that happened today...

1._____
2._____
3._____

How could I have made today even better?

_____

What would make tomorrow really great?

_____
_____

Date ___/___/20___

"Don't let others do your thinking." ~ Joseph Murphy

I am grateful for....

1._____
2._____
3._____

What empowered belief will I adopt to replace a limiting belief that has held me back?

_____

What healthy choice would make today really great?

_____

Daily Affirmations. I am....

_____
_____
_____

3 Amazing things that happened today...

1._____
2._____
3._____

How could I have made today even better?

_____

What would make tomorrow really great?

_____
_____

Date ___/___/20___

"Promise me you'll always remember: You're braver than you believe, and stronger than you seem, and smarter than you think."

~ Christopher Robin

I am grateful for....

1._____
2._____
3._____

What empowered belief will I adopt to replace a limiting belief that has held me back?

_____

What healthy choice would make today really great?

_____

Daily Affirmations. I am....

_____
_____
_____

3 Amazing things that happened today...

1._____
2._____
3._____

How could I have made today even better?

_____

What would make tomorrow really great?

_____
_____

Date ___/___/20___

"A happy life consists not in the absence, but in the mastery of hardships." ~ Helen Keller

I am grateful for....

1._____
2._____
3._____

What empowered belief will I adopt to replace a limiting belief that has held me back?

_____

What healthy choice would make today really great?

_____

Daily Affirmations. I am....

_____
_____

3 Amazing things that happened today...

1._____
2._____
3._____

How could I have made today even better?

_____

What would make tomorrow really great?

_____

Date ___/___/20___

"It is better to be hated for what you are than to be loved for what you are not." ~ Andre Gide

I am grateful for....

1._____
2._____
3._____

What empowered belief will I adopt to replace a limiting belief that has held me back?

_____

What healthy choice would make today really great?

_____

Daily Affirmations. I am....

_____

_____

3 Amazing things that happened today...

1._____
2._____
3._____

How could I have made today even better?

_____

What would make tomorrow really great?

_____

Date ___/___/20___

9"Think twice before you speak, because your words and influence will plant the seed of either success or failure in the mind of another." ~ Napolean Hill

I am grateful for....

1._____
2._____
3._____

What empowered belief will I adopt to replace a limiting belief that has held me back?

_____

What healthy choice would make today really great?

_____

Daily Affirmations. I am....

_____
_____

3 Amazing things that happened today...

1._____
2._____
3._____

How could I have made today even better?

_____

What would make tomorrow really great?

_____
_____

Date ___/___/20___

"What you think, feel, and do is what you see, hear, and attract."
~ James Altucher

I am grateful for....

1._____
2._____
3._____

What empowered belief will I adopt to replace a limiting belief that has held me back?

_____

What healthy choice would make today really great?

_____

Daily Affirmations. I am....

_____
_____

3 Amazing things that happened today...

1._____
2._____
3._____

How could I have made today even better?

_____

What would make tomorrow really great?

_____
_____

Date ___/___/20___

"If it isn't moving you toward your goal, then trade it for something that will." ~ Sheila (Day) Shaver

I am grateful for....

1._____
2._____
3._____

What empowered belief will I adopt to replace a limiting belief that has held me back?

_____

What healthy choice would make today really great?

_____

Daily Affirmations. I am....

_____
_____
_____

3 Amazing things that happened today...

1._____
2._____
3._____

How could I have made today even better?

_____

What would make tomorrow really great?

_____
_____

Date ___/___/20___

"Gratitude is riches. Complaint is poverty." ~ Doris Day

I am grateful for....

1._____
2._____
3._____

What empowered belief will I adopt to replace a limiting belief that has held me back?

_____

What healthy choice would make today really great?

_____

Daily Affirmations. I am....

_____
_____

3 Amazing things that happened today...

1._____
2._____
3._____

How could I have made today even better?

_____

What would make tomorrow really great?

_____

Date ___/___/20___

"Exercise is king. Nutrition is queen. Put them together and you've got a kingdom." ~ Jack LeLanne

I am grateful for....

1._____
2._____
3._____

What empowered belief will I adopt to replace a limiting belief that has held me back?

_____

What healthy choice would make today really great?

_____

Daily Affirmations. I am....

_____
_____

3 Amazing things that happened today...

1._____
2._____
3._____

How could I have made today even better?

_____

What would make tomorrow really great?

_____
_____

Date ___/___/20___

"If you do what you've always done, you'll get what you've always gotten." ~ Tony Robbins

I am grateful for....

1._____
2._____
3._____

What empowered belief will I adopt to replace a limiting belief that has held me back?

_____

What healthy choice would make today really great?

_____

Daily Affirmations. I am....

_____
_____
_____

3 Amazing things that happened today...

1._____
2._____
3._____

How could I have made today even better?

_____

What would make tomorrow really great?

_____
_____

Date ___/___/20___

"Do what is easy and your life will be hard. Do what is hard and your life will be easy." ~ Les Brown

I am grateful for....

1._____
2._____
3._____

What empowered belief will I adopt to replace a limiting belief that has held me back?

_____

What healthy choice would make today really great?

_____

Daily Affirmations. I am....

_____
_____
_____

3 Amazing things that happened today...

1._____
2._____
3._____

How could I have made today even better?

_____

What would make tomorrow really great?

_____
_____

Date ___/___/20___

"Your outside world is a reflection of your inside world. What goes on in the inside, shows on the outside." ~ Bob Proctor

I am grateful for....

1._____

2._____

3._____

What empowered belief will I adopt to replace a limiting belief that has held me back?

_____

What healthy choice would make today really great?

_____

Daily Affirmations. I am....

_____

_____

_____

3 Amazing things that happened today...

1._____

2._____

3._____

How could I have made today even better?

_____

What would make tomorrow really great?

_____

_____

Date ___/___/20___

"What a wonderful life I've had! I only wish I'd realized it sooner." ~ Sidonie-Gabrielle Colette

I am grateful for....

1._____
2._____
3._____

What empowered belief will I adopt to replace a limiting belief that has held me back?

_____

What healthy choice would make today really great?

_____

Daily Affirmations. I am....

_____
_____
_____

3 Amazing things that happened today...

1._____
2._____
3._____

How could I have made today even better?

_____

What would make tomorrow really great?

_____

Date ___/___/20___

"If you spend your whole life waiting for the storm, you'll never enjoy the sunshine." ~ Morris West

I am grateful for....

1._____
2._____
3._____

What empowered belief will I adopt to replace a limiting belief that has held me back?

_____

What healthy choice would make today really great?

_____

Daily Affirmations. I am....

_____
_____
_____

3 Amazing things that happened today...

1._____
2._____
3._____

How could I have made today even better?

_____

What would make tomorrow really great?

_____
_____

Date ___/___/20___

"Gratitude opens the door to the power, the wisdom, the creativity of the universe. You open the door through gratitude."
~ Deepak Chopra

I am grateful for....

1._____
2._____
3._____

What empowered belief will I adopt to replace a limiting belief that has held me back?

_____

What healthy choice would make today really great?

_____

Daily Affirmations. I am....

_____
_____
_____

3 Amazing things that happened today...

1._____
2._____
3._____

How could I have made today even better?

_____

What would make tomorrow really great?

_____
_____

"It's the repetition of affirmations that leads to belief. And once that belief becomes a deep conviction, things begin to happen."

~ Muhammad Ali

I am grateful for....

1._____
2._____
3._____

What empowered belief will I adopt to replace a limiting belief that has held me back?

_____

What healthy choice would make today really great?

_____

Daily Affirmations. I am....

_____
_____
_____

3 Amazing things that happened today...

1._____
2._____
3._____

How could I have made today even better?

_____

What would make tomorrow really great?

_____
_____

Date ___/___/20___

"Whatever the conscious, reasoning mind of man believes, the subconscious mind will accept and act upon." ~ Joseph Murphy

I am grateful for....

1._____
2._____
3._____

What empowered belief will I adopt to replace a limiting belief that has held me back?

_____

What healthy choice would make today really great?

_____

Daily Affirmations. I am....

_____
_____
_____

3 Amazing things that happened today...

1._____
2._____
3._____

How could I have made today even better?

_____

What would make tomorrow really great?

_____
_____

Date ___/___/20___

"To keep the body in good health is a duty, otherwise we shall not be able to keep our minds strong and clear." ~ Buddha

I am grateful for....

1._____
2._____
3._____

What empowered belief will I adopt to replace a limiting belief that has held me back?

_____

What healthy choice would make today really great?

_____

Daily Affirmations. I am....

_____
_____
_____

3 Amazing things that happened today...

1._____
2._____
3._____

How could I have made today even better?

_____

What would make tomorrow really great?

_____
_____

Date ___/___/20___

"And the day came when the risk to remain tight in a bud was more painful than the risk it took to blossom." ~ Elizabeth Appel

I am grateful for....

1._____
2._____
3._____

What empowered belief will I adopt to replace a limiting belief that has held me back?

_____

What healthy choice would make today really great?

_____

Daily Affirmations. I am....

_____
_____
_____

3 Amazing things that happened today...

1._____
2._____
3._____

How could I have made today even better?

_____

What would make tomorrow really great?

_____
_____

Date ___/___/20___

"Do not follow where the path may lead. Go instead where there is no path and leave a trail." ~ Doug Larson

I am grateful for....

1._____
2._____
3._____

What empowered belief will I adopt to replace a limiting belief that has held me back?

_____

What healthy choice would make today really great?

_____

Daily Affirmations. I am....

_____
_____
_____

3 Amazing things that happened today...

1._____
2._____
3._____

How could I have made today even better?

_____

What would make tomorrow really great?

_____
_____

Date ___/___/20___

"Vision is not enough; it must be combined with venture. It is not enough to stare up the steps; we must step up the stairs."

~ Vaclav Havel.

I am grateful for....

1._____
2._____
3._____

What empowered belief will I adopt to replace a limiting belief that has held me back?

_____

What healthy choice would make today really great?

_____

Daily Affirmations. I am....

_____
_____
_____

3 Amazing things that happened today...

1._____
2._____
3._____

How could I have made today even better?

_____

What would make tomorrow really great?

_____
_____

Date ___/___/20___

I am grateful for....

1._____
2._____
3._____

What empowered belief will I adopt to replace a limiting belief that has held me back?

_____

What healthy choice would make today really great?

_____

Daily Affirmations. I am....

_____
_____
_____

3 Amazing things that happened today...

1._____
2._____
3._____

How could I have made today even better?

_____

What would make tomorrow really great?

_____
_____

Date ___/___/20___

"The key to becoming world-class in your endeavors is to build your performance around world-class routines."
~ Darren Hardy

I am grateful for....

1._____
2._____
3._____

What empowered belief will I adopt to replace a limiting belief that has held me back?

_____

What healthy choice would make today really great?

_____

Daily Affirmations. I am....

_____
_____
_____

3 Amazing things that happened today...

1._____
2._____
3._____

How could I have made today even better?

_____

What would make tomorrow really great?

_____
_____

Date ___/___/20___

"The first step towards success is taken when you refuse to be a captive of the environment in which you first find yourself."
~ Mark Caine

I am grateful for....

1._____
2._____
3._____

What empowered belief will I adopt to replace a limiting belief that has held me back?

_____

What healthy choice would make today really great?

_____

Daily Affirmations. I am....

_____
_____
_____

3 Amazing things that happened today...

1._____
2._____
3._____

How could I have made today even better?

_____

What would make tomorrow really great?

_____
_____

Date ___/___/20___

"You get what you tolerate. If you tolerate mediocre, that's exactly what you will get." ~ Tony Robbins

I am grateful for....

1._____
2._____
3._____

What empowered belief will I adopt to replace a limiting belief that has held me back?

_____

What healthy choice would make today really great?

_____

Daily Affirmations. I am....

_____
_____
_____

3 Amazing things that happened today...

1._____
2._____
3._____

How could I have made today even better?

_____

What would make tomorrow really great?

_____

Date ___/___/20___

"Life is ten percent what happens to you and ninety percent how you respond to it." ~ Charles Swindoll

I am grateful for....

1._____
2._____
3._____

What empowered belief will I adopt to replace a limiting belief that has held me back?

_____

What healthy choice would make today really great?

_____

Daily Affirmations. I am....

_____
_____
_____

3 Amazing things that happened today...

1._____
2._____
3._____

How could I have made today even better?

_____

What would make tomorrow really great?

_____
_____

Date ___/___/20___

"When we lose sight of ourselves and see past our limitations, only then will we success." ~ Scott Shaver

I am grateful for....

1._____

2._____

3._____

What empowered belief will I adopt to replace a limiting belief that has held me back?

_____

What healthy choice would make today really great?

_____

Daily Affirmations. I am....

_____

_____

_____

3 Amazing things that happened today...

1._____

2._____

3._____

How could I have made today even better?

_____

What would make tomorrow really great?

_____

_____

Date ___/___/20___

I am grateful for....

1._____
2._____
3._____

What empowered belief will I adopt to replace a limiting belief that has held me back?

_____

What healthy choice would make today really great?

_____

Daily Affirmations. I am....

_____

_____

_____

3 Amazing things that happened today...

1._____
2._____
3._____

How could I have made today even better?

_____

What would make tomorrow really great?

_____

_____

Date ___/___/20___

"If you want to get to the next level of whatever you're doing, you must think and act in a wildly different way than you previously have been."

~ Grant Cardone

I am grateful for....

1._____
2._____
3._____

What empowered belief will I adopt to replace a limiting belief that has held me back?

_____

What healthy choice would make today really great?

_____

Daily Affirmations. I am....

_____
_____
_____

3 Amazing things that happened today...

1._____
2._____
3._____

How could I have made today even better?

_____

What would make tomorrow really great?

_____
_____

Date ___/___/20___

"A successful man is one who can lay a firm foundation with the bricks others have thrown at him." ~ David Brinkley

I am grateful for....

1._____
2._____
3._____

What empowered belief will I adopt to replace a limiting belief that has held me back?

_____

What healthy choice would make today really great?

_____

Daily Affirmations. I am....

_____
_____
_____

3 Amazing things that happened today...

1._____
2._____
3._____

How could I have made today even better?

_____

What would make tomorrow really great?

_____

Date ___/___/20___

"Those who dare to fail miserably can achieve greatly."
~ John F. Kennedy

I am grateful for....

1._____
2._____
3._____

What empowered belief will I adopt to replace a limiting belief
that has held me back?

_____

What healthy choice would make today really great?

_____

Daily Affirmations. I am....

_____
_____

3 Amazing things that happened today...

1._____
2._____
3._____

How could I have made today even better?

_____

What would make tomorrow really great?

_____

Date ___/ ___/20___

"In minds crammed with thoughts, organs clogged with toxins, and bodies stiffened with neglect, there is just no space for anything else."
~ Alison Rose Levy

I am grateful for....

1._____
2._____
3._____

What empowered belief will I adopt to replace a limiting belief that has held me back?

_____

What healthy choice would make today really great?

_____

Daily Affirmations. I am....

_____
_____
_____

3 Amazing things that happened today...

1._____
2._____
3._____

How could I have made today even better?

_____

What would make tomorrow really great?

_____
_____

Date ___/___/20___

"It had long since come to my attention that people of accomplishment rarely set back and let things happen to them. They went out and happened to things." ~ Leonardo da Vinci

I am grateful for....

1._____
2._____
3._____

What empowered belief will I adopt to replace a limiting belief that has held me back?

_____

What healthy choice would make today really great?

_____

Daily Affirmations. I am....

_____
_____

3 Amazing things that happened today...

1._____
2._____
3._____

How could I have made today even better?

_____

What would make tomorrow really great?

_____
_____

Date ___/___/20___

"If you want to achieve excellence, you can get there today. As of this second, quit doing less-than-excellent work."

~ Thomas J. Watson

I am grateful for....

1._____
2._____
3._____

What empowered belief will I adopt to replace a limiting belief that has held me back?

_____

What healthy choice would make today really great?

_____

Daily Affirmations. I am....

_____
_____

3 Amazing things that happened today...

1._____
2._____
3._____

How could I have made today even better?

_____

What would make tomorrow really great?

_____
_____

Date ___/___/20___

"If you want to live a happy life, tie it to a goal and not to people or things." ~ Albert Einstein

I am grateful for....

1._____
2._____
3._____

What empowered belief will I adopt to replace a limiting belief that has held me back?

_____

What healthy choice would make today really great?

_____

Daily Affirmations. I am....

_____
_____
_____

3 Amazing things that happened today...

1._____
2._____
3._____

How could I have made today even better?

_____

What would make tomorrow really great?

_____

Date ___/___/20___

"Turn your face to the sun and the shadows fall behind you."
~ Maori Proverb

I am grateful for....

1._____
2._____
3._____

What empowered belief will I adopt to replace a limiting belief that has held me back?

_____

What healthy choice would make today really great?

_____

Daily Affirmations. I am....

_____
_____

3 Amazing things that happened today...

1._____
2._____
3._____

How could I have made today even better?

_____

What would make tomorrow really great?

_____
_____

Date ___/___/20___

"The opposite of love is not hate, it is indifference." ~ Elie Wiesel

I am grateful for....

1._____
2._____
3._____

What empowered belief will I adopt to replace a limiting belief that has held me back?

_____

What healthy choice would make today really great?

_____

Daily Affirmations. I am....

_____
_____
_____

3 Amazing things that happened today...

1._____
2._____
3._____

How could I have made today even better?

_____

What would make tomorrow really great?

_____
_____

Date ___/___/20___

"Walking is the best possible exercise. Habituate yourself to walk very far." ~ Thomas Jefferson

I am grateful for....

1._____
2._____
3._____

What empowered belief will I adopt to replace a limiting belief that has held me back?

_____

What healthy choice would make today really great?

_____

Daily Affirmations. I am....

_____
_____
_____

3 Amazing things that happened today...

1._____
2._____
3._____

How could I have made today even better?

_____

What would make tomorrow really great?

_____
_____

Date ___/___/20___

"As you saw in your subconscious mind, so shall you reap in your body and environment." ~ Joseph Murphy

I am grateful for....

1._____
2._____
3._____

What empowered belief will I adopt to replace a limiting belief that has held me back?

_____

What healthy choice would make today really great?

_____

Daily Affirmations. I am....

_____
_____

3 Amazing things that happened today...

1._____
2._____
3._____

How could I have made today even better?

_____

What would make tomorrow really great?

_____

Date ___/___/20___

"Let gratitude be the pillow upon which you kneel to say your nightly prayer." ~ Maya Angelou

I am grateful for....

1._____
2._____
3._____

What empowered belief will I adopt to replace a limiting belief that has held me back?

_____

What healthy choice would make today really great?

_____

Daily Affirmations. I am....

_____
_____

3 Amazing things that happened today...

1._____
2._____
3._____

How could I have made today even better?

_____

What would make tomorrow really great?

_____
_____

Date ___/___/20___

"If you don't design your own life plan, chances are you'll fall into someone else's plan. And guess what they have planned for you? Not much."

~ Jim Rohn

I am grateful for....

1._____
2._____
3._____

What empowered belief will I adopt to replace a limiting belief that has held me back?

_____

What healthy choice would make today really great?

_____

Daily Affirmations. I am....

_____
_____

3 Amazing things that happened today...

1._____
2._____
3._____

How could I have made today even better?

_____

What would make tomorrow really great?

_____
_____

Date ___/___/20___

"The patient should be made to understand that he or she must take charge of his own life. Don't take your body to the doctor as if he were a repair shop."

~ Quentin Regestein

I am grateful for....

1._____
2._____
3._____

What empowered belief will I adopt to replace a limiting belief that has held me back?

_____

What healthy choice would make today really great?

_____

Daily Affirmations. I am....

_____
_____

3 Amazing things that happened today...

1._____
2._____
3._____

How could I have made today even better?

_____

What would make tomorrow really great?

_____
_____

Date ___/___/20___

"Always be a first-rate version of yourself and not a second-rate version of someone else." ~ Judy Garland

I am grateful for....

1._____
2._____
3._____

What empowered belief will I adopt to replace a limiting belief that has held me back?

_____

What healthy choice would make today really great?

_____

Daily Affirmations. I am....

_____

_____

3 Amazing things that happened today...

1._____
2._____
3._____

How could I have made today even better?

_____

What would make tomorrow really great?

_____

_____

Date ___/___/20___

"In the end, only three things matter: how much you loved, how gently you lived, and how gracefully you let go of things not meant for you." ~ Buddha

I am grateful for....

1._____
2._____
3._____

What empowered belief will I adopt to replace a limiting belief that has held me back?

_____

What healthy choice would make today really great?

_____

Daily Affirmations. I am....

_____
_____

3 Amazing things that happened today...

1._____
2._____
3._____

How could I have made today even better?

_____

What would make tomorrow really great?

_____
_____

Date ___/___/20___

"The question isn't 'Who is going to let me' it's 'Who is going to stop me.'" ~ Ayn Rand

I am grateful for....

1._____
2._____
3._____

What empowered belief will I adopt to replace a limiting belief that has held me back?

_____

What healthy choice would make today really great?

_____

Daily Affirmations. I am....

_____
_____
_____

3 Amazing things that happened today...

1._____
2._____
3._____

How could I have made today even better?

_____

What would make tomorrow really great?

_____
_____

Date ___/___/20___

"Gratitude doesn't change the scenery. It merely washes clean the glass you look through so you can clearly see the colors."
~ Richelle E. Goodrich

I am grateful for....

1._____
2._____
3._____

What empowered belief will I adopt to replace a limiting belief that has held me back?

_____

What healthy choice would make today really great?

_____

Daily Affirmations. I am....

_____

_____

_____

3 Amazing things that happened today...

1._____
2._____
3._____

How could I have made today even better?

_____

What would make tomorrow really great?

_____

_____

Date ___/___/20___

"Any psychologist will tell you that healing comes form honest confrontation with our injury or with our past. Whatever that thing is that hurt us or traumatized us, until we face it head on, we will have issues moving forward in a healthy way." ~ Nate Parker

I am grateful for....

1._____
2._____
3._____

What empowered belief will I adopt to replace a limiting belief that has held me back?

_____

What healthy choice would make today really great?

_____

Daily Affirmations. I am....

_____
_____
_____

3 Amazing things that happened today...

1._____
2._____
3._____

How could I have made today even better?

_____

What would make tomorrow really great?

_____
_____

Date ___/___/20___

"You have been assigned this mountain so you can show others it can be moved." ~ Mel Robbins

I am grateful for....

1._____
2._____
3._____

What empowered belief will I adopt to replace a limiting belief that has held me back?

_____

What healthy choice would make today really great?

_____

Daily Affirmations. I am....

_____
_____
_____

3 Amazing things that happened today...

1._____
2._____
3._____

How could I have made today even better?

_____

What would make tomorrow really great?

_____
_____

Date ___/___/20___

"Spread love everywhere you go. Let no one ever come to you without leaving happier." ~ Mother Teresa

I am grateful for....

1._____
2._____
3._____

What empowered belief will I adopt to replace a limiting belief that has held me back?

_____

What healthy choice would make today really great?

_____

Daily Affirmations. I am....

_____
_____
_____

3 Amazing things that happened today...

1._____
2._____
3._____

How could I have made today even better?

_____

What would make tomorrow really great?

_____
_____

Date ___/___/20___

"Don't be pushed by your problems, be led by your dreams."
~ Ralph Waldo Emerson

I am grateful for....

1._____
2._____
3._____

What empowered belief will I adopt to replace a limiting belief that has held me back?

_____

What healthy choice would make today really great?

_____

Daily Affirmations. I am....

_____
_____

3 Amazing things that happened today...

1._____
2._____
3._____

How could I have made today even better?

_____

What would make tomorrow really great?

_____
_____

Date ___/___/20___

"Happiness can be found in even the darkest of times, but only to those who remember to turn on the light." ~ J.K. Rowling

I am grateful for....

1._____
2._____
3._____

What empowered belief will I adopt to replace a limiting belief that has held me back?

_____

What healthy choice would make today really great?

_____

Daily Affirmations. I am....

_____
_____
_____

3 Amazing things that happened today...

1._____
2._____
3._____

How could I have made today even better?

_____

What would make tomorrow really great?

_____

Date ___/___/20___

"You must be the change you wish to see in the world." ~ Ghandhi

I am grateful for....

1._____
2._____
3._____

What empowered belief will I adopt to replace a limiting belief that has held me back?

_____

What healthy choice would make today really great?

_____

Daily Affirmations. I am....

_____
_____

3 Amazing things that happened today...

1._____
2._____
3._____

How could I have made today even better?

_____

What would make tomorrow really great?

_____
_____

Date ___/___/20___

"Whatever the problem, be part of the solution. Don't just sit around raising questions and pointing out obstacles." ~ Tina Fey

I am grateful for....

1._____
2._____
3._____

What empowered belief will I adopt to replace a limiting belief that has held me back?

_____

What healthy choice would make today really great?

_____

Daily Affirmations. I am....

_____
_____

3 Amazing things that happened today...

1._____
2._____
3._____

How could I have made today even better?

_____

What would make tomorrow really great?

_____

Date ___/___/20___

"Get busy living, or get busy dying." ~ Stephen King

I am grateful for....

1._____
2._____
3._____

What empowered belief will I adopt to replace a limiting belief that has held me back?

_____

What healthy choice would make today really great?

_____

Daily Affirmations. I am....

_____
_____

3 Amazing things that happened today...

1._____
2._____
3._____

How could I have made today even better?

_____

What would make tomorrow really great?

_____
_____

Date ___/___/20___

"Every step taken in mindfulness brings us one step closer to healing ourselves and the planet." ~Thich Nhat Hahn

I am grateful for....

1._____
2._____
3._____

What empowered belief will I adopt to replace a limiting belief that has held me back?

_____

What healthy choice would make today really great?

_____

Daily Affirmations. I am....

_____
_____
_____

3 Amazing things that happened today...

1._____
2._____
3._____

How could I have made today even better?

_____

What would make tomorrow really great?

_____
_____

Date ___/___/20___

"Natural forces within us are the true healers. Let your food be your medicine and let your medicine be your food." ~ Hippocrates

I am grateful for....

1._____
2._____
3._____

What empowered belief will I adopt to replace a limiting belief that has held me back?

_____

What healthy choice would make today really great?

_____

Daily Affirmations. I am....

_____
_____
_____

3 Amazing things that happened today...

1._____
2._____
3._____

How could I have made today even better?

_____

What would make tomorrow really great?

_____

Date ___/___/20___

"Whatever you vividly imagine, ardently desire, sincerely believe, and enthusiastically act upon…must inevitably come to pass~" ~
Darren Hardy

I am grateful for….

1._____
2._____
3._____

What empowered belief will I adopt to replace a limiting belief that has held me back?

_____

What healthy choice would make today really great?

_____

Daily Affirmations. I am….

_____

_____

_____

3 Amazing things that happened today…

1._____
2._____
3._____

How could I have made today even better?

_____

What would make tomorrow really great?

_____

_____

Date ___/___/20___

"We make our decisions, and then our decisions turn around and make us." ~ F.W. Boreham

I am grateful for....

1._____
2._____
3._____

What empowered belief will I adopt to replace a limiting belief that has held me back?

_____

What healthy choice would make today really great?

_____

Daily Affirmations. I am....

_____

_____

_____

3 Amazing things that happened today...

1._____
2._____
3._____

How could I have made today even better?

_____

What would make tomorrow really great?

_____

_____

Date ___/___/20___

"Vitality and beauty are gifts of nature for those who live according to its laws." ~ Leonardo da Vinci

I am grateful for....

1._____
2._____
3._____

What empowered belief will I adopt to replace a limiting belief that has held me back?

_____

What healthy choice would make today really great?

_____

Daily Affirmations. I am....

_____
_____

3 Amazing things that happened today...

1._____
2._____
3._____

How could I have made today even better?

_____

What would make tomorrow really great?

_____
_____

Date ___/___/20___

"When we focus on gratitude, the tide of disappointment goes out and the tide of love rushes in." ~ Kristin Armstrong

I am grateful for....

1._____
2._____
3._____

What empowered belief will I adopt to replace a limiting belief that has held me back?

_____

What healthy choice would make today really great?

_____

Daily Affirmations. I am....

_____
_____

3 Amazing things that happened today...

1._____
2._____
3._____

How could I have made today even better?

_____

What would make tomorrow really great?

_____
_____

Date ___/___/20___

"The art of living lies less in eliminating our troubles than in growing with them." ~ Bernard Baruch

I am grateful for....

1._____
2._____
3._____

What empowered belief will I adopt to replace a limiting belief that has held me back?

_____

What healthy choice would make today really great?

_____

Daily Affirmations. I am....

_____
_____
_____

3 Amazing things that happened today...

1._____
2._____
3._____

How could I have made today even better?

_____

What would make tomorrow really great?

_____

Date ___/___/20___

"And you ask "What if I fall?" Oh, but my darling, what if you fly?" ~ Erin Hanson

I am grateful for....

1._____
2._____
3._____

What empowered belief will I adopt to replace a limiting belief that has held me back?

_____

What healthy choice would make today really great?

_____

Daily Affirmations. I am....

_____
_____
_____

3 Amazing things that happened today...

1._____
2._____
3._____

How could I have made today even better?

_____

What would make tomorrow really great?

_____
_____

Date ___/___/20___

"Trade your expectation for appreciation and the world changes for you." ~ Tony Robbins

I am grateful for....

1._____
2._____
3._____

What empowered belief will I adopt to replace a limiting belief that has held me back?

_____

What healthy choice would make today really great?

_____

Daily Affirmations. I am....

_____
_____
_____

3 Amazing things that happened today...

1._____
2._____
3._____

How could I have made today even better?

_____

What would make tomorrow really great?

_____
_____

Date ___/___/20___

"The difference between the impossible and the possible lies in a person's determination." ~ Tommy Lasorda

I am grateful for....

1._____
2._____
3._____

What empowered belief will I adopt to replace a limiting belief that has held me back?

_____

What healthy choice would make today really great?

_____

Daily Affirmations. I am....

_____
_____
_____

3 Amazing things that happened today...

1._____
2._____
3._____

How could I have made today even better?

_____

What would make tomorrow really great?

_____
_____

Date ___/___/20___

"As we express our gratitude, we must never forget that the highest appreciation is not to utter words, but to live by them."
~ John F. Kennedy

I am grateful for....

1._____
2._____
3._____

What empowered belief will I adopt to replace a limiting belief that has held me back?

_____

What healthy choice would make today really great?

_____

Daily Affirmations. I am....

_____
_____
_____

3 Amazing things that happened today...

1._____
2._____
3._____

How could I have made today even better?

_____

What would make tomorrow really great?

_____
_____

Date ___/___/20___

"The journey of a thousand miles begins with one step." ~ Lao Tzu

I am grateful for....

1._____
2._____
3._____

What empowered belief will I adopt to replace a limiting belief that has held me back?

_____

What healthy choice would make today really great?

_____

Daily Affirmations. I am....

_____

_____

3 Amazing things that happened today...

1._____
2._____
3._____

How could I have made today even better?

_____

What would make tomorrow really great?

_____

Date ___/___/20___

"Life isn't about finding yourself, life is about creating yourself."
~ George Bernand Shaw

I am grateful for....

1._____
2._____
3._____

What empowered belief will I adopt to replace a limiting belief that has held me back?

_____

What healthy choice would make today really great?

_____

Daily Affirmations. I am....

_____
_____

3 Amazing things that happened today...

1._____
2._____
3._____

How could I have made today even better?

_____

What would make tomorrow really great?

_____
_____

Date ___/___/20___

"Success is not final, failure is not fatal: It is the courage to continue that counts." ~ Winston Churchill

I am grateful for....

1._____
2._____
3._____

What empowered belief will I adopt to replace a limiting belief that has held me back?

_____

What healthy choice would make today really great?

_____

Daily Affirmations. I am....

_____
_____
_____

3 Amazing things that happened today...

1._____
2._____
3._____

How could I have made today even better?

_____

What would make tomorrow really great?

_____

Date ___/___/20___

"Your time is limited so don't waste it living someone else's life. Don't be trapped by dogma - which is living with the results of other people's thinking."
~ Steve Jobs

I am grateful for....

1._____
2._____
3._____

What empowered belief will I adopt to replace a limiting belief that has held me back?

_____

What healthy choice would make today really great?

_____

Daily Affirmations. I am....

_____
_____

3 Amazing things that happened today...

1._____
2._____
3._____

How could I have made today even better?

_____

What would make tomorrow really great?

_____
_____

Date ___/___/20___

"It's not what you do some of the time that counts, it's what you do all of the time that counts." ~ Jack LaLanne

I am grateful for....

1._____
2._____
3._____

What empowered belief will I adopt to replace a limiting belief that has held me back?

_____

What healthy choice would make today really great?

_____

Daily Affirmations. I am....

_____
_____
_____

3 Amazing things that happened today...

1._____
2._____
3._____

How could I have made today even better?

_____

What would make tomorrow really great?

_____
_____

Date ___/___/20___

"When we are no longer able to change a situation, we are challenged to change ourselves." Viktor Frankl

I am grateful for....

1._____
2._____
3._____

What empowered belief will I adopt to replace a limiting belief that has held me back?

_____

What healthy choice would make today really great?

_____

Daily Affirmations. I am....

_____
_____
_____

3 Amazing things that happened today...

1._____
2._____
3._____

How could I have made today even better?

_____

What would make tomorrow really great?

_____
_____

Date ___/___/20___

"Love yourself first and everything else falls into line. You really have to love yourself to get anything done in this world."
~ Lucille Ball

I am grateful for....

1._____
2._____
3._____

What empowered belief will I adopt to replace a limiting belief that has held me back?

_____

What healthy choice would make today really great?

_____

Daily Affirmations. I am....

_____
_____

3 Amazing things that happened today...

1._____
2._____
3._____

How could I have made today even better?

_____

What would make tomorrow really great?

_____
_____

Date ___/___/20___

"If we don't change, we don't grow. If we don't grow, we are not really living. Growth demands a temporary surrender of security."
~ Gail Sheehy

I am grateful for....

1._____
2._____
3._____

What empowered belief will I adopt to replace a limiting belief that has held me back?

_____

What healthy choice would make today really great?

_____

Daily Affirmations. I am....

_____

_____

_____

3 Amazing things that happened today...

1._____
2._____
3._____

How could I have made today even better?

_____

What would make tomorrow really great?

_____

_____

Date ___/___/20___

"Many of life's failures are people who did not realize how close they were to success when they gave up." ~ Thomas A. Edison

I am grateful for....

1._____
2._____
3._____

What empowered belief will I adopt to replace a limiting belief that has held me back?

_____

What healthy choice would make today really great?

_____

Daily Affirmations. I am....

_____
_____
_____

3 Amazing things that happened today...

1._____
2._____
3._____

How could I have made today even better?

_____

What would make tomorrow really great?

_____
_____

Date ___/___/20___

"You miss a hundred percent of the shots you never take."
~ Wayne Gretzky

I am grateful for....

1._____

2._____

3._____

What empowered belief will I adopt to replace a limiting belief that has held me back?

_____

What healthy choice would make today really great?

_____

Daily Affirmations. I am....

_____

_____

3 Amazing things that happened today...

1._____

2._____

3._____

How could I have made today even better?

_____

What would make tomorrow really great?

_____

_____

Date ___/___/20___

"You bring out the best in yourself by looking for the best in others." ~ Gene Bedley

I am grateful for....

1._____
2._____
3._____

What empowered belief will I adopt to replace a limiting belief that has held me back?

_____

What healthy choice would make today really great?

_____

Daily Affirmations. I am....

_____
_____
_____

3 Amazing things that happened today...

1._____
2._____
3._____

How could I have made today even better?

_____

What would make tomorrow really great?

_____
_____

Date ___/___/20___

"A ship is safe in harbor, but that's not what ships are for."
~ John A. Shedd

I am grateful for....

1._____
2._____
3._____

What empowered belief will I adopt to replace a limiting belief that has held me back?

_____

What healthy choice would make today really great?

_____

Daily Affirmations. I am....

_____

_____

3 Amazing things that happened today...

1._____
2._____
3._____

How could I have made today even better?

_____

What would make tomorrow really great?

_____

_____

Date ___/___/20___

"Remove those "I want you to like me" stickers from your forehead and, instead, place them where they truly will do the most good – on your mirror!"

~ Susan Jeffers

I am grateful for....

1._____
2._____
3._____

What empowered belief will I adopt to replace a limiting belief that has held me back?

_____

What healthy choice would make today really great?

_____

Daily Affirmations. I am....

_____
_____
_____

3 Amazing things that happened today...

1._____
2._____
3._____

How could I have made today even better?

_____

What would make tomorrow really great?

_____
_____

Date ___/___/20___

"Remember that the happiest people are not those getting more but those giving more." ~ H. Jackson Brown Jr.

I am grateful for....

1._____
2._____
3._____

What empowered belief will I adopt to replace a limiting belief that has held me back?

_____

What healthy choice would make today really great?

_____

Daily Affirmations. I am....

_____
_____

3 Amazing things that happened today...

1._____
2._____
3._____

How could I have made today even better?

_____

What would make tomorrow really great?

_____

Date ___/___/20___

"Too many of us are not living our dreams because we are living our fears." ~ Les Brown

I am grateful for....

1._____
2._____
3._____

What empowered belief will I adopt to replace a limiting belief that has held me back?

_____

What healthy choice would make today really great?

_____

Daily Affirmations. I am....

_____
_____

3 Amazing things that happened today...

1._____
2._____
3._____

How could I have made today even better?

_____

What would make tomorrow really great?

_____

Date ___/___/20___

"Faith and fear both demand you believe in something you cannot see. You choose." ~ Bob Proctor

I am grateful for....

1._____
2._____
3._____

What empowered belief will I adopt to replace a limiting belief that has held me back?

_____

What healthy choice would make today really great?

_____

Daily Affirmations. I am....

_____
_____
_____

3 Amazing things that happened today...

1._____
2._____
3._____

How could I have made today even better?

_____

What would make tomorrow really great?

_____
_____

Date ___/ ___/20___

"Thought is cause, experience is effect. If you don't like the effects in your life, you have to changes the nature of your thinking."

~ Marianne Williamson

I am grateful for....

1._____
2._____
3._____

What empowered belief will I adopt to replace a limiting belief that has held me back?

_____

What healthy choice would make today really great?

_____

Daily Affirmations. I am....

_____
_____
_____

3 Amazing things that happened today...

1._____
2._____
3._____

How could I have made today even better?

_____

What would make tomorrow really great?

_____
_____

Date ___/___/20___

"Happiness is when what you think, what you say, and what you do are in harmony." ~ Gandhi

I am grateful for....

1._____
2._____
3._____

What empowered belief will I adopt to replace a limiting belief that has held me back?

_____

What healthy choice would make today really great?

_____

Daily Affirmations. I am....

_____
_____
_____

3 Amazing things that happened today...

1._____
2._____
3._____

How could I have made today even better?

_____

What would make tomorrow really great?

_____

Date ___/___/20___

"There is no stress in the world, only people thinking stressful thoughts and acting on them." ~ Dr. Wayne Dyer

I am grateful for....

1._____
2._____
3._____

What empowered belief will I adopt to replace a limiting belief that has held me back?

_____

What healthy choice would make today really great?

_____

Daily Affirmations. I am....

_____
_____

3 Amazing things that happened today...

1._____
2._____
3._____

How could I have made today even better?

_____

What would make tomorrow really great?

_____
_____

Date ___/___/20___

"I can be changed by what happens to me, but I refuse to be reduced by it." ~ Maya Angelou

I am grateful for....

1._____
2._____
3._____

What empowered belief will I adopt to replace a limiting belief that has held me back?

_____

What healthy choice would make today really great?

_____

Daily Affirmations. I am....

_____
_____
_____

3 Amazing things that happened today...

1._____
2._____
3._____

How could I have made today even better?

_____

What would make tomorrow really great?

_____

Date ___/___/20___

"Until you value yourself you will not value your time. Until you value your time, you will not do anything with it." ~ M. Scott Peck

I am grateful for....

1._____
2._____
3._____

What empowered belief will I adopt to replace a limiting belief that has held me back?

_____

What healthy choice would make today really great?

_____

Daily Affirmations. I am....

_____
_____
_____

3 Amazing things that happened today...

1._____
2._____
3._____

How could I have made today even better?

_____

What would make tomorrow really great?

_____

Date ___/___/20___

"Every morning when you wake up, determine to be the best you that you can be." ~ Sheila (Day) Shaver

I am grateful for....

1._____
2._____
3._____

What empowered belief will I adopt to replace a limiting belief that has held me back?

_____

What healthy choice would make today really great?

_____

Daily Affirmations. I am....

_____
_____
_____

3 Amazing things that happened today...

1._____
2._____
3._____

How could I have made today even better?

_____

What would make tomorrow really great?

_____
_____

Date ___/___/20___

"Things may come to those who wait, but only the things left by those who hustle." ~ Abraham Lincoln

I am grateful for....

1._____
2._____
3._____

What empowered belief will I adopt to replace a limiting belief that has held me back?

_____

What healthy choice would make today really great?

_____

Daily Affirmations. I am....

_____
_____

3 Amazing things that happened today...

1._____
2._____
3._____

How could I have made today even better?

_____

What would make tomorrow really great?

_____

Date ___/___/20___

"To accomplish great things, we must dream as well as act."
~ Anatole France

I am grateful for....

1._____
2._____
3._____

What empowered belief will I adopt to replace a limiting belief that has held me back?

_____

What healthy choice would make today really great?

_____

Daily Affirmations. I am....

_____
_____

3 Amazing things that happened today...

1._____
2._____
3._____

How could I have made today even better?

_____

What would make tomorrow really great?

_____
_____

Date ___/___/20___

"The successful warrior is the average man, with laser-like focus." ~
Bruce Lee

I am grateful for....

1._____
2._____
3._____

What empowered belief will I adopt to replace a limiting belief
that has held me back?

_____

What healthy choice would make today really great?

_____

Daily Affirmations. I am....

_____

_____

3 Amazing things that happened today...

1._____
2._____
3._____

How could I have made today even better?

_____

What would make tomorrow really great?

_____

_____

Date ___/___/20___

"Don't be afraid of the storms, for that is where you learn to sail."
~ Sheila (Day) Shaver

I am grateful for....

1._____
2._____
3._____

What empowered belief will I adopt to replace a limiting belief that has held me back?

_____

What healthy choice would make today really great?

_____

Daily Affirmations. I am....

_____
_____

3 Amazing things that happened today...

1._____
2._____
3._____

How could I have made today even better?

_____

What would make tomorrow really great?

_____
_____

Date ___/___/20___

"You can't depend on your eyes when your imagination is out of focus." ~ Mark Twain

I am grateful for....

1._____
2._____
3._____

What empowered belief will I adopt to replace a limiting belief that has held me back?

_____

What healthy choice would make today really great?

_____

Daily Affirmations. I am....

_____

_____

_____

3 Amazing things that happened today...

1._____
2._____
3._____

How could I have made today even better?

_____

What would make tomorrow really great?

_____

_____

Date ___/___/20___

"If you don't stick to your values when they are being tested, they're not values; they're hobbies." ~ Jon Stewart

I am grateful for....

1._____
2._____
3._____

What empowered belief will I adopt to replace a limiting belief that has held me back?

_____

What healthy choice would make today really great?

_____

Daily Affirmations. I am....

_____
_____

3 Amazing things that happened today...

1._____
2._____
3._____

How could I have made today even better?

_____

What would make tomorrow really great?

_____
_____

Date ___/___/20___

"God can take the good, the bad, and the bitter and create a masterpiece called your destiny." ~ Tony Evans

I am grateful for....

1._____
2._____
3._____

What empowered belief will I adopt to replace a limiting belief that has held me back?

_____

What healthy choice would make today really great?

_____

Daily Affirmations. I am....

_____
_____

3 Amazing things that happened today...

1._____
2._____
3._____

How could I have made today even better?

_____

What would make tomorrow really great?

_____
_____

Date ___/___/20___

"A person's success in life can usually be measured by the number of uncomfortable conversations he or she is willing to have."
~ Tim Ferriss

I am grateful for....

1._____
2._____
3._____

What empowered belief will I adopt to replace a limiting belief that has held me back?

_____

What healthy choice would make today really great?

_____

Daily Affirmations. I am....

_____
_____
_____

3 Amazing things that happened today...

1._____
2._____
3._____

How could I have made today even better?

_____

What would make tomorrow really great?

_____
_____

"Having limits to push against is how you find out what you can do." ~ Sylvie Guillem

I am grateful for....

1._____
2._____
3._____

What empowered belief will I adopt to replace a limiting belief that has held me back?

_____

What healthy choice would make today really great?

_____

Daily Affirmations. I am....

_____

_____

3 Amazing things that happened today...

1._____
2._____
3._____

How could I have made today even better?

_____

What would make tomorrow really great?

_____

_____

Date ___/___/20___

"He who lives in harmony with himself lives in harmony with the universe." ~ Marcus Aurelius

I am grateful for....

1._____
2._____
3._____

What empowered belief will I adopt to replace a limiting belief that has held me back?

_____

What healthy choice would make today really great?

_____

Daily Affirmations. I am....

_____

_____

3 Amazing things that happened today...

1._____
2._____
3._____

How could I have made today even better?

_____

What would make tomorrow really great?

_____

Date ___/___/20___

"A small behavioural change can also lead to embracing a wider checklist of healthier choices." ~ Chuck Norris

I am grateful for....

1._____
2._____
3._____

What empowered belief will I adopt to replace a limiting belief that has held me back?

_____

What healthy choice would make today really great?

_____

Daily Affirmations. I am....

_____
_____
_____

3 Amazing things that happened today...

1._____
2._____
3._____

How could I have made today even better?

_____

What would make tomorrow really great?

_____

Date ___/___/20___

"The only person you are destined to become is the person you decide to be." ~ Ralph Waldo Emerson

I am grateful for....

1._____
2._____
3._____

What empowered belief will I adopt to replace a limiting belief that has held me back?

_____

What healthy choice would make today really great?

_____

Daily Affirmations. I am....

_____
_____
_____

3 Amazing things that happened today...

1._____
2._____
3._____

How could I have made today even better?

_____

What would make tomorrow really great?

_____
_____

Date ___/___/20___

"Often when you think you're at the end of something, you're at the beginning of something else." ~ Fred Rogers

I am grateful for....

1._____
2._____
3._____

What empowered belief will I adopt to replace a limiting belief that has held me back?

_____

What healthy choice would make today really great?

_____

Daily Affirmations. I am....

_____
_____
_____

3 Amazing things that happened today...

1._____
2._____
3._____

How could I have made today even better?

_____

What would make tomorrow really great?

_____
_____

Date ___/___/20___

"The ultimate measure of a man is not where he stands in moments of comfort and convenience, but where he stands at times of challenge and controversy."
~ Martin Luther King

I am grateful for....

1._____
2._____
3._____

What empowered belief will I adopt to replace a limiting belief that has held me back?

_____

What healthy choice would make today really great?

_____

Daily Affirmations. I am....

_____
_____

3 Amazing things that happened today...

1._____
2._____
3._____

How could I have made today even better?

_____

What would make tomorrow really great?

_____
_____

Date ___/___/20___

"There is nothing noble in being superior to your fellow man; true nobility is being superior to your former self." ~ Ernest Hemingway

I am grateful for....

1._____
2._____
3._____

What empowered belief will I adopt to replace a limiting belief that has held me back?

_____

What healthy choice would make today really great?

_____

Daily Affirmations. I am....

_____
_____

3 Amazing things that happened today...

1._____
2._____
3._____

How could I have made today even better?

_____

What would make tomorrow really great?

_____

Date ___/___/20___

"There is only one success: To be able to spend your life in your way." ~ Christopher Morley

I am grateful for....

1._____
2._____
3._____

What empowered belief will I adopt to replace a limiting belief that has held me back?

_____

What healthy choice would make today really great?

_____

Daily Affirmations. I am....

_____

_____

3 Amazing things that happened today...

1._____
2._____
3._____

How could I have made today even better?

_____

What would make tomorrow really great?

_____

_____

Date ___/___/20___

"The fastest way to change yourself is to hang out with people who are already the way you want to be." ~ Ben Casnocha

I am grateful for....

1._____
2._____
3._____

What empowered belief will I adopt to replace a limiting belief that has held me back?

_____

What healthy choice would make today really great?

_____

Daily Affirmations. I am....

_____

_____

_____

3 Amazing things that happened today...

1._____
2._____
3._____

How could I have made today even better?

_____

What would make tomorrow really great?

_____

Date ___/___/20___

"First you have to believe in yourself before others can believe in you." ~ Mimi Ikonn

I am grateful for....

1._____
2._____
3._____

What empowered belief will I adopt to replace a limiting belief that has held me back?

_____

What healthy choice would make today really great?

_____

Daily Affirmations. I am....

_____
_____
_____

3 Amazing things that happened today...

1._____
2._____
3._____

How could I have made today even better?

_____

What would make tomorrow really great?

_____

Date ___/___/20___

"The only thing that's keeping you from getting what you want is the story you keep telling yourself." ~ Tony Robbins

I am grateful for....

1._____
2._____
3._____

What empowered belief will I adopt to replace a limiting belief that has held me back?

_____

What healthy choice would make today really great?

_____

Daily Affirmations. I am....

_____
_____

3 Amazing things that happened today...

1._____
2._____
3._____

How could I have made today even better?

_____

What would make tomorrow really great?

_____

Date ___/___/20___

"You don't have to be great to get started, but you have to get started to be great." ~ Les Brown

I am grateful for....

1._____
2._____
3._____

What empowered belief will I adopt to replace a limiting belief that has held me back?

_____

What healthy choice would make today really great?

_____

Daily Affirmations. I am....

_____
_____

3 Amazing things that happened today...

1._____
2._____
3._____

How could I have made today even better?

_____

What would make tomorrow really great?

_____
_____

Date ___/___/20___

"Gratitude can transform common days into thanksgivings, turn routine jobs into joy, and change ordinary opportunities into blessings."

~ William Arthur Ward

I am grateful for....

1._____
2._____
3._____

What empowered belief will I adopt to replace a limiting belief that has held me back?

_____

What healthy choice would make today really great?

_____

Daily Affirmations. I am....

_____

_____

_____

3 Amazing things that happened today...

1._____
2._____
3._____

How could I have made today even better?

_____

What would make tomorrow really great?

_____

_____

Date ___/___/20___

"Do not be misled, bad company corrupts good character."
~ 1 Cor: 15:33

I am grateful for....

1._____
2._____
3._____

What empowered belief will I adopt to replace a limiting belief that has held me back?

_____

What healthy choice would make today really great?

_____

Daily Affirmations. I am....

_____
_____

3 Amazing things that happened today...

1._____
2._____
3._____

How could I have made today even better?

_____

What would make tomorrow really great?

_____
_____

Date ___/___/20___

"Walk with the wise and become wise, for a companion of fools suffers harm." ~ Prov 13:20

I am grateful for....

1._____
2._____
3._____

What empowered belief will I adopt to replace a limiting belief that has held me back?

_____

What healthy choice would make today really great?

_____

Daily Affirmations. I am....

_____
_____
_____

3 Amazing things that happened today...

1._____
2._____
3._____

How could I have made today even better?

_____

What would make tomorrow really great?

_____
_____

Date ___/___/20___

"Gratitude turns what we have into enough, and more. It turns denial into acceptance, chaos into order, confusion into clarity - it makes sense of our past, brings peace for today, and creates a vision for tomorrow."~ Melody Beattie

I am grateful for....

1._____
2._____
3._____

What empowered belief will I adopt to replace a limiting belief that has held me back?

_____

What healthy choice would make today really great?

_____

Daily Affirmations. I am....

_____
_____
_____

3 Amazing things that happened today...

1._____
2._____
3._____

How could I have made today even better?

_____

What would make tomorrow really great?

_____
_____

Date ___/___/20___

"I attribute my success to this: I never gave or took any excuse."
~ Florence Nightingale

I am grateful for....

1._____
2._____
3._____

What empowered belief will I adopt to replace a limiting belief that has held me back?

_____

What healthy choice would make today really great?

_____

Daily Affirmations. I am....

_____
_____

3 Amazing things that happened today...

1._____
2._____
3._____

How could I have made today even better?

_____

What would make tomorrow really great?

_____
_____

Date ___/___/20___

"Yesterday I was clever, so I wanted to change the world. Today I am wise, so I am changing myself." ~ Rumi

I am grateful for....

1._____
2._____
3._____

What empowered belief will I adopt to replace a limiting belief that has held me back?

_____

What healthy choice would make today really great?

_____

Daily Affirmations. I am....

_____
_____

3 Amazing things that happened today...

1._____
2._____
3._____

How could I have made today even better?

_____

What would make tomorrow really great?

_____

Date ___/___/20___

"Postpone joy, it will diminish. Postpone a problem, and it will grow." ~ Paulo Coelho

I am grateful for....

1._____
2._____
3._____

What empowered belief will I adopt to replace a limiting belief that has held me back?

_____

What healthy choice would make today really great?

_____

Daily Affirmations. I am....

_____

_____

_____

3 Amazing things that happened today...

1._____
2._____
3._____

How could I have made today even better?

_____

What would make tomorrow really great?

_____

_____

Date ___/___/20___

"Success is often achieved by those who don't know that failure is inevitable." ~ Coco Chanel

I am grateful for....

1._____
2._____
3._____

What empowered belief will I adopt to replace a limiting belief that has held me back?

_____

What healthy choice would make today really great?

_____

Daily Affirmations. I am....

_____
_____
_____

3 Amazing things that happened today...

1._____
2._____
3._____

How could I have made today even better?

_____

What would make tomorrow really great?

_____
_____

Date ___/___/20___

"Successful people decide how they are going to live; they are not victims of circumstance. In good times or bad times, they know where they are going and they know that they are going to get there." ~ Bob Proctor

I am grateful for....

1._____
2._____
3._____

What empowered belief will I adopt to replace a limiting belief that has held me back?

_____

What healthy choice would make today really great?

_____

Daily Affirmations. I am....

_____

_____

3 Amazing things that happened today...

1._____
2._____
3._____

How could I have made today even better?

_____

What would make tomorrow really great?

_____

_____

Date ___/___/20___

"The world as we have created it is a process of our thinking. It cannot be changed without changing our thinking."
~ Albert Einstein

I am grateful for....

1._____
2._____
3._____

What empowered belief will I adopt to replace a limiting belief that has held me back?

_____

What healthy choice would make today really great?

_____

Daily Affirmations. I am....

_____
_____

3 Amazing things that happened today...

1._____
2._____
3._____

How could I have made today even better?

_____

What would make tomorrow really great?

_____
_____

Date ___/___/20___

"Those who cannot change their minds cannot change anything." ~
George Bernard Shaw

I am grateful for....

1._____
2._____
3._____

What empowered belief will I adopt to replace a limiting belief
that has held me back?

_____

What healthy choice would make today really great?

_____

Daily Affirmations. I am....

_____

_____

3 Amazing things that happened today...

1._____
2._____
3._____

How could I have made today even better?

_____

What would make tomorrow really great?

_____

_____

Date ___/___/20___

"I alone cannot change the world, but I can cast a stone across the waters to create many ripples." ~ Mother Teresa

I am grateful for....

1._____
2._____
3._____

What empowered belief will I adopt to replace a limiting belief that has held me back?

_____

What healthy choice would make today really great?

_____

Daily Affirmations. I am....

_____
_____
_____

3 Amazing things that happened today...

1._____
2._____
3._____

How could I have made today even better?

_____

What would make tomorrow really great?

_____
_____

Date ___/___/20___

"To improve is to change; to be perfect is to change often."
~ Winston Churchill

I am grateful for....

1._____
2._____
3._____

What empowered belief will I adopt to replace a limiting belief that has held me back?

_____

What healthy choice would make today really great?

_____

Daily Affirmations. I am....

_____
_____

3 Amazing things that happened today...

1._____
2._____
3._____

How could I have made today even better?

_____

What would make tomorrow really great?

_____
_____

Date ___/___/20___

I am grateful for....

1._____
2._____
3._____

What empowered belief will I adopt to replace a limiting belief that has held me back?

_____

What healthy choice would make today really great?

_____

Daily Affirmations. I am....

_____

_____

3 Amazing things that happened today...

1._____
2._____
3._____

How could I have made today even better?

_____

What would make tomorrow really great?

_____

_____

Date ___/___/20___

"As a man thinketh in his heart, so is he." ~ Prov 23:7

I am grateful for....

1._____
2._____
3._____

What empowered belief will I adopt to replace a limiting belief
that has held me back?

_____

What healthy choice would make today really great?

_____

Daily Affirmations. I am....

_____
_____
_____

3 Amazing things that happened today...

1._____
2._____
3._____

How could I have made today even better?

_____

What would make tomorrow really great?

_____
_____

Date ___/___/20___

"It's only after you have stepped outside your comfort zone that you begin to change, grow, and transform." ~ Roy T. Bennett

I am grateful for....

1._____
2._____
3._____

What empowered belief will I adopt to replace a limiting belief that has held me back?

_____

What healthy choice would make today really great?

_____

Daily Affirmations. I am....

_____
_____
_____

3 Amazing things that happened today...

1._____
2._____
3._____

How could I have made today even better?

_____

What would make tomorrow really great?

_____
_____

Date ___/___/20___

"It's not the situation that's causing your stress, its' your thoughts, and you can change that right here and now. You can choose to be peaceful right here and now. Peace is a choice, and it has nothing to do with what other people do or think." ~ Gerald G. Jampolsky, MD

I am grateful for....

1._____
2._____
3._____

What empowered belief will I adopt to replace a limiting belief that has held me back?

_____

What healthy choice would make today really great?

_____

Daily Affirmations. I am....

_____
_____

3 Amazing things that happened today...

1._____
2._____
3._____

How could I have made today even better?

_____

What would make tomorrow really great?

_____
_____

Date ___/___/20___

"Take responsibility for your own happiness, never put it in other people's hands." ~ Roy T. Bennett

I am grateful for....

1._____
2._____
3._____

What empowered belief will I adopt to replace a limiting belief that has held me back?

_____

What healthy choice would make today really great?

_____

Daily Affirmations. I am....

_____
_____
_____

3 Amazing things that happened today...

1._____
2._____
3._____

How could I have made today even better?

_____

What would make tomorrow really great?

_____
_____

Date ___/___/20___

"Don't waste your time with explanations, people only hear what they want to hear." ~ Paulo Coelho

I am grateful for....

1._____
2._____
3._____

What empowered belief will I adopt to replace a limiting belief that has held me back?

_____

What healthy choice would make today really great?

_____

Daily Affirmations. I am....

_____
_____

3 Amazing things that happened today...

1._____
2._____
3._____

How could I have made today even better?

_____

What would make tomorrow really great?

_____

Date ___/___/20___

"You yourself, as much as anybody in the entire universe, deserve your love and affection." ~ Sharon Salzberg

I am grateful for....

1._____
2._____
3._____

What empowered belief will I adopt to replace a limiting belief that has held me back?

_____

What healthy choice would make today really great?

_____

Daily Affirmations. I am....

_____
_____
_____

3 Amazing things that happened today...

1._____
2._____
3._____

How could I have made today even better?

_____

What would make tomorrow really great?

_____
_____

Date ___/___/20___

"You are today where your thoughts have brought you; you will be tomorrow where your thoughts take you." ~ James Allen

I am grateful for....

1._____
2._____
3._____

What empowered belief will I adopt to replace a limiting belief that has held me back?

_____

What healthy choice would make today really great?

_____

Daily Affirmations. I am....

_____
_____
_____

3 Amazing things that happened today...

1._____
2._____
3._____

How could I have made today even better?

_____

What would make tomorrow really great?

_____
_____

Date ___/___/20___

"The significant problems we face in life cannot be solved at the same level of thinking we were at when we created them."

~ Albert Einstein

I am grateful for....

1._____
2._____
3._____

What empowered belief will I adopt to replace a limiting belief that has held me back?

_____

What healthy choice would make today really great?

_____

Daily Affirmations. I am....

_____
_____
_____

3 Amazing things that happened today...

1._____
2._____
3._____

How could I have made today even better?

_____

What would make tomorrow really great?

_____
_____

Date ___/___/20___

"You have powers you never dreamed of. You can do things you never thoughts you could do. There are no limitations in what you can do except the limitations of your own mind." ~ Darwin P. Kingsley

I am grateful for....

1._____
2._____
3._____

What empowered belief will I adopt to replace a limiting belief that has held me back?

_____

What healthy choice would make today really great?

_____

Daily Affirmations. I am....

_____

_____

_____

3 Amazing things that happened today...

1._____
2._____
3._____

How could I have made today even better?

_____

What would make tomorrow really great?

_____

_____

Date ___/___/20___

"Men are not prisoners of fate, but only prisoners of their own minds." ~ Franklin D. Roosevelt

I am grateful for....

1._____
2._____
3._____

What empowered belief will I adopt to replace a limiting belief that has held me back?

_____

What healthy choice would make today really great?

_____

Daily Affirmations. I am....

_____
_____
_____

3 Amazing things that happened today...

1._____
2._____
3._____

How could I have made today even better?

_____

What would make tomorrow really great?

_____
_____

Date ___/___/20___

"Man's power of choice enables him to think like an angel or a devil, a king or a slave. Whatever he chooses, his mind will create and manifest." ~
Frederick Bailes

I am grateful for....

1._____
2._____
3._____

What empowered belief will I adopt to replace a limiting belief that has held me back?

_____

What healthy choice would make today really great?

_____

Daily Affirmations. I am....

_____
_____

3 Amazing things that happened today...

1._____
2._____
3._____

How could I have made today even better?

_____

What would make tomorrow really great?

_____
_____

Date ___/___/20___

"Remember, happiness doesn't depend upon who you are or what you have; it depends solely upon what you think." ~ Dale Carnegie

I am grateful for....

1._____
2._____
3._____

What empowered belief will I adopt to replace a limiting belief that has held me back?

_____

What healthy choice would make today really great?

_____

Daily Affirmations. I am....

_____
_____
_____

3 Amazing things that happened today...

1._____
2._____
3._____

How could I have made today even better?

_____

What would make tomorrow really great?

_____
_____

Date ___/___/20___

"The game of life is the game of boomerangs. Our thoughts, deeds and words return to us sooner or later, with astounding accuracy." ~ Florence Shinn

I am grateful for....

1._____
2._____
3._____

What empowered belief will I adopt to replace a limiting belief that has held me back?

_____

What healthy choice would make today really great?

_____

Daily Affirmations. I am....

_____
_____

3 Amazing things that happened today...

1._____
2._____
3._____

How could I have made today even better?

_____

What would make tomorrow really great?

_____
_____

You have two weeks left to journal in this book,
And in two weeks you will have completed six months
Of new transformational habits.

If you have found this experiment to be transformational,
Then keep going and see what you can accomplish.

Share with a friend or family member who
You would love to see transform their life too.

Time To Reorder

Please make sure you write to us to share
The transformations you have experienced
The past six months of journaling.

7minutetransformationaljournal@gmail.com

Date ___/___/20___

"Focus on understanding yourself instead of blaming others."
~ Wayne Dyer

I am grateful for....

1._____
2._____
3._____

What empowered belief will I adopt to replace a limiting belief that has held me back?

_____

What healthy choice would make today really great?

_____

Daily Affirmations. I am....

_____
_____

3 Amazing things that happened today...

1._____
2._____
3._____

How could I have made today even better?

_____

What would make tomorrow really great?

_____
_____

Date ___/___/20___

I am grateful for....

1._____
2._____
3._____

What empowered belief will I adopt to replace a limiting belief that has held me back?

_____

What healthy choice would make today really great?

_____

Daily Affirmations. I am....

_____

_____

3 Amazing things that happened today...

1._____
2._____
3._____

How could I have made today even better?

_____

What would make tomorrow really great?

_____

_____

Date ___/___/20___

"If you change the way you look at things, the things you look at change." ~ Wayne Dyer

I am grateful for....

1._____
2._____
3._____

What empowered belief will I adopt to replace a limiting belief that has held me back?

_____

What healthy choice would make today really great?

_____

Daily Affirmations. I am....

_____
_____
_____

3 Amazing things that happened today...

1._____
2._____
3._____

How could I have made today even better?

_____

What would make tomorrow really great?

_____
_____

Date ___/___/20___

"Incredible change happens in your life when you decide to take control of what you do have power over instead of craving control over what you don't."
~ Steve Maraboli

I am grateful for....

1._____
2._____
3._____

What empowered belief will I adopt to replace a limiting belief that has held me back?

_____

What healthy choice would make today really great?

_____

Daily Affirmations. I am....

_____
_____

3 Amazing things that happened today...

1._____
2._____
3._____

How could I have made today even better?

_____

What would make tomorrow really great?

_____
_____

Date ___/___/20___

"The most authentic thing about us is our capacity to create, to overcome, to endure, to transform, to love, and to be greater than our suffering."

~ Ben Okri

I am grateful for....

1._____

2._____

3._____

What empowered belief will I adopt to replace a limiting belief that has held me back?

_____

What healthy choice would make today really great?

_____

Daily Affirmations. I am....

_____

_____

_____

3 Amazing things that happened today...

1._____

2._____

3._____

How could I have made today even better?

_____

What would make tomorrow really great?

_____

_____

Date ___/___/20___

"Life will only change when you become more committed to your dreams than you are to your comfort zone." ~ Billy Cox

I am grateful for....

1._____
2._____
3._____

What empowered belief will I adopt to replace a limiting belief that has held me back?

_____

What healthy choice would make today really great?

_____

Daily Affirmations. I am....

_____

_____

3 Amazing things that happened today...

1._____
2._____
3._____

How could I have made today even better?

_____

What would make tomorrow really great?

_____

"Sometimes it takes a good fall to know where you really stand."
~ Hayley Williams

I am grateful for....

1._____
2._____
3._____

What empowered belief will I adopt to replace a limiting belief that has held me back?

_____

What healthy choice would make today really great?

_____

Daily Affirmations. I am....

_____

_____

3 Amazing things that happened today...

1._____
2._____
3._____

How could I have made today even better?

_____

What would make tomorrow really great?

_____

_____

Date ___/___/20___

"Your emotions are the slaves to your thoughts, and you are the slaves to your emotions." ~ Elizabeth Gilbert

I am grateful for....

1._____
2._____
3._____

What empowered belief will I adopt to replace a limiting belief that has held me back?

_____

What healthy choice would make today really great?

_____

Daily Affirmations. I am....

_____
_____
_____

3 Amazing things that happened today...

1._____
2._____
3._____

How could I have made today even better?

_____

What would make tomorrow really great?

_____
_____

Date ___/___/20___

"In any given moment we have two options; to step forward into growth or to step back into safety." ~ Abraham Maslow

I am grateful for....

1._____
2._____
3._____

What empowered belief will I adopt to replace a limiting belief that has held me back?

_____

What healthy choice would make today really great?

_____

Daily Affirmations. I am....

_____

_____

3 Amazing things that happened today...

1._____
2._____
3._____

How could I have made today even better?

_____

What would make tomorrow really great?

_____

Date ___/___/20___

"The pessimist complains about the wind; the optimist expects it to change; the realist adjusts the sails." ~ William Arthur Ward

I am grateful for....

1._____
2._____
3._____

What empowered belief will I adopt to replace a limiting belief that has held me back?

_____

What healthy choice would make today really great?

_____

Daily Affirmations. I am....

_____
_____

3 Amazing things that happened today...

1._____
2._____
3._____

How could I have made today even better?

_____

What would make tomorrow really great?

_____

Date ___/___/20___

"When the winds of change blow, some people build walls and others build windmills." ~ Chinese proverb

I am grateful for....

1._____
2._____
3._____

What empowered belief will I adopt to replace a limiting belief that has held me back?

_____

What healthy choice would make today really great?

_____

Daily Affirmations. I am....

_____

_____

_____

3 Amazing things that happened today...

1._____
2._____
3._____

How could I have made today even better?

_____

What would make tomorrow really great?

_____

_____

Date ___/___/20___

"God's timing is always perfect. Trust His delays. He's got you."
~ Tony Evans

I am grateful for....

1._____
2._____
3._____

What empowered belief will I adopt to replace a limiting belief that has held me back?

_____

What healthy choice would make today really great?

_____

Daily Affirmations. I am....

_____
_____

3 Amazing things that happened today...

1._____
2._____
3._____

How could I have made today even better?

_____

What would make tomorrow really great?

_____
_____

"The world is waiting for you to wake up to the person you are called to be. Stop listening to the negative inner conversation that's causing you to play small." ~ Les Brown

I am grateful for....

1._____
2._____
3._____

What empowered belief will I adopt to replace a limiting belief that has held me back?

_____

What healthy choice would make today really great?

_____

Daily Affirmations. I am....

_____

_____

3 Amazing things that happened today...

1._____
2._____
3._____

How could I have made today even better?

_____

What would make tomorrow really great?

_____

_____

Date ___/___/20___

"Everything you put into your mind, body, spirit offers you either health or dis-ease, success or failure, life or death. There is no middle ground."

~ Sheila (Day) Shaver

I am grateful for....

1._____
2._____
3._____

What empowered belief will I adopt to replace a limiting belief that has held me back?

_____

What healthy choice would make today really great?

_____

Daily Affirmations. I am....

_____
_____

3 Amazing things that happened today...

1._____
2._____
3._____

How could I have made today even better?

_____

What would make tomorrow really great?

_____
_____

Made in the
USA
Monee, IL